Speaking with **Spirit**

A Guide for Christian Public Speakers

Speaking with **Spirit**
A Guide for Christian Public Speakers

DR. WANDA VASSALLO

AMBASSADOR INTERNATIONAL
Greenville, South Carolina • Belfast, Northern Ireland

Speaking with Spirit:
A Guide for Christian Public Speakers

Unless otherwise indicated, all Scriptural references are from The New King James Version.

Cover design & page layout by A & E Media—Paula Shepherd

ISBN 1 889893 85 4

Published by the Ambassador Group

Ambassador Emerald International
427 Wade Hampton Blvd.
Greenville, SC 29609
USA
www.emeraldhouse.com

and

Ambassador Publications Ltd.
Providence House
Ardenlee Street
Belfast BT6 8QJ
Northern Ireland
www.ambassador-productions.com

The colophon is a trademark of Ambassador

For Rick and Laurie, who grew up in the audience
and were often part of the act

CONTENTS

Preview ix

Chapter One 1
Jesus as a Speaker—Our Example

Chapter Two 15
Making Friends with Your Worst Enemy—You!

Chapter Three 27
Presenting Yourself as a Speaker

Chapter Four 41
The Mechanics of Speaking

Chapter Five 59
Connecting with Your Audience

Chapter Six 85
Show and Tell Your Message

Chapter Seven 105
Writing the Speech

Chapter Eight 129
Getting Ready for the Big Event

Chapter Nine 137
Sixteen Types of Speeches

Chapter Ten 177
Conducting Meetings

Chapter Eleven 189
So You're Going to Be on Television

Chapter Twelve 203
Getting Organized as a Speaker

Appendix 1: Review 213
Appendix 2: Speaking the Scriptures 217
Endnotes 221
Index 229

Endorsements

"This extraordinary piece of work is the most thorough treatment on the subject of public speaking I have ever seen. *Speaking with Spirit* is full of factual information organized in easily recognizable categories. I was particularly gratified to find not only a catalog of possible openings for different types of speeches but also an example of each taken from a successful presentation. When you have finished Wanda's book, you will regard speaking before an audience as something to anticipate with confidence and optimism."

—LINUS WRIGHT, *Former Under Secretary, U.S. Department of Education, and Dallas Schools Superintendent*

"At last! A public speaking book written especially for Christian speakers. Wanda's book will serve as a trusted guide for the novice speaker as well as a valuable reference for the experienced speaker cast onto unfamiliar turf, such as appearing on television for the first time. Her examples of different genres of speeches, tailor-made for Christian audiences, provide a treasure trove of proven material."

—MAMIE MCCULLOUGH, *Motivational Speaker and Author*

"I am so pleased that Wanda has written another book on speaking. Her previous book on the subject proved to be very popular at our conferences. We sold several hundred copies. Wanda has spoken at our conferences over the years and has always been a favorite among our people. I know this book will be well received. I am eager to begin offering it to our conference attendees."

—REG A. FORDER, *Director of American Christian Writers*

"This book by Wanda Vassallo will be much appreciated and used by pastors and leaders in Christian churches, as well as by speakers in other contexts. Having served as a pastor for 28 years, as well as being a theological educator and a denominational executive, I am called on to speak in a variety of settings. Based on my experiences, I know that Wanda's book will be a priceless resource for the Christian leader. I recommend it without reservation."

—REV. RONALD E. VALLET, *D.Min., Author, Adjunct Professor, McMaster Divinity College; Pastor, Fredonia Baptist Church, Fredonia, N.Y.; Minister for Stewardship and Mission Support, American Baptist Churches of New York.*

"I taught Communications in a Christian University for many years and often used Jesus Christ as an example of the greatest of the communicators. Naturally, I directed my students to scriptures that verified that fact, but I never had a complete scriptural reference to Christ's sermons, teachings, speeches, and arguments. Now, Wanda Vassallo has included in her first-rate public speaking textbook, a chapter on "Jesus as a Speaker--Our Example!" This is a true blessing for the Christian speech teacher. It's all there in Dr. Vassallo's book-- all the scripture references, the interpretations of those scriptures, and the speech "techniques" of Christ! It's all there in a textbook that goes on to tell the student and the teacher how best to present oneself before an audience. It's all there in one volume--a complete course in public speaking. A text like this with Jesus as the master speaker has long been needed. Now, it's available. Our prayers have been answered. Thank you, Dr. Wanda Vassallo!"

—DR. ROSE-MARY RUMBLEY, *University Professor, Professional Speaker, and Author*

Preview

Connecting with an audience and feeling as though you've made an impact on people is an exciting experience. It's also addictive.

I found that out at the very early age of five. Since I was a very shy child, my mother had given me "expression" lessons to help overcome my timidity. Now I was facing my first recital. I had rehearsed and rehearsed and rehearsed my eight-line poem with all the pre-programmed gestures and appropriate facial expressions. I knew exactly how to walk to the platform, face the audience, and begin with my first line.

All that carefully rehearsed preparation went out the window, however, when I arrived center stage and saw my older brother in the front row of the audience broadly grinning up at me. I thought he was making fun of me. I was furious. I threw timidity to the wind, placed my hands on my hips, and shouted at him: "Junior, if you don't stop laughing at me, I'm going to throw you in the garbage can!"

The audience roared with laughter. I didn't realize they were laughing at me. I only knew that I loved the sensation of being able to make all those people respond to something I had said—bizarre as it was. I still haven't gotten over the love affair I developed that day with an audience.

Fortunately, my parents, my church, and my teachers encouraged my fascination with the spoken word throughout my school years.

When it came time to go to college, I decided to major in speech and drama. I taught speech, drama, and music at all levels in the public schools for several years. The next leg of my journey with speaking took me to a different form of speaking. I served as Coordinator of Instructional Television with the Mesquite (Texas) schools and did program planning as well as acted as the storybook lady for two children's television literature series. During that time, I went back to school to earn a master's degree with a minor in speech and drama and a major in audiovisual education, which proved to be intricately related to and helpful in speaking.

After completing that degree, I found myself on the other side of the speaker's stand, putting my years of experience and training in public speaking to good use as speechwriter for the Superintendent of the Dallas schools for 12 years. I also led public speaking sessions and workshops for adults and taught speech for a home school association.

Through the years I have given about every kind of speech you can imagine—everything from Sunday school lessons and musical reviews to entertaining speeches and workshops. As you can imagine, I gathered heaps of material along the way.

I recently completed a Doctor of Ministry degree with an emphasis on the use of drama in the church.

One day I sat down and thought, "Speaking well is so important. What I've learned and experienced along the way surely could help others who want to do a better job as public speakers." So I wrote a book—one like the book I wished I had had when I first started teaching public speaking. Published as *Speaking with Confidence* by Betterway Books in 1990, the book fared well, being designated by the American Library Association as "a must for an excellent collection of books of this genre".

When it was taken out of print in 2000, I thought it would be exciting to rewrite it as a book especially for speakers who are Christians. So here it is with a new look and a new title, *Speaking with Spirit*.

To me, what is intriguing about being a speaker is that there's always room for improvement, and that each audience is a new, exhilarating challenge. I hope this book will prove helpful as you seek to make an impact in the lives of others as a Christian public speaker.

Blessings,
Wanda Vassallo, D. Min.

Chapter 1

JESUS AS A SPEAKER—OUR EXAMPLE

*For the Holy Spirit will teach you in that very hour what you
ought to say (Luke 12:12).*

Talk about encouraging words! Those inspiring words of Jesus tell
us that, as Christian speakers, we don't have to do it all on our own.

Not only do we have His words of encouragement, but we
also have His example as a speaker, revealed in the four Gospels.

Only a tiny sample of Jesus' three years of ministry is available to
us today. Herman Harrell Horne wrote: "…all the incidents reported
in the Gospels fall on only 35 days over a period of some three years."[1]
In John 21:25 we read: "And there are also many other things that
Jesus did, which if they were written one by one, I suppose that even
the world itself could not contain the books that would be written."

With no media coverage of His teachings, no video or audio
tapes, and no computers—or even printing presses—to record what
He said, it's amazing that His words and approaches to speaking
survived. That they are available to us today is a testament to His
power and impact as a speaker.

How wonderful it would be to have a video of Jesus giving the
Sermon on the Mount! No doubt we could learn much of value
about His manner and style from such a recording. But we can
also learn from studying the four Gospels from the standpoint of a
student of public speaking.

Jesus' Approaches as a Speaker

When we look at what Jesus did as a speaker, we see several
main characteristics.

- Jesus did not call attention to Himself, but to His message.
- Jesus spoke what God told Him to say. He looked to God for wisdom and for the ordering of His thoughts.
- He did not talk down to His listeners. He identified himself as the "son of man." In doing so, He related to His listeners by becoming one of them. He did not take a distant, superior stance.
- He was humble. There was no trace of self-exaltation in His words or approach.
- He spoke with authority. No one could describe Him as a timid speaker.
- He was direct.
- He did not soft-pedal what He had to say to make His message "acceptable."
- His vocal projection and clarity of speech enabled Him to speak to "multitudes" on a mountaintop (Matt. 5:1), from a boat in a lake to "multitudes" on the shore (Matt. 13:2), and to five thousand in a desert place (Matt. 14:14-15).
- He had an excellent command of language.
- He was extraordinary as an impromptu speaker, seizing on a topic or event of the moment and elaborating on the subject as He went.
- He was aware of the importance of the comfort and well-being of His listeners as evidenced by the fact that He fed a crowd of five thousand men, plus women and children.
- Jesus' teaching was positive, emphasizing the commands beginning "You shall…" over "You shall not…" He came "not to abolish but to fulfill" (Matt. 5:17).
- His message was inclusive—for everyone, regardless of gender, nationality, or background.

Emphasis on Inclusion

Fortunately, today's trend is to try to use inclusive language and examples in communicating so that no one feels left out. That trend was definitely not present in Jesus' day. The prevailing culture was distinctly critical of and negative toward anyone deemed to be "other." Jesus' insistence on including the outcasts of Palestinian culture shocked and enraged the establishment. He did not hesitate to proclaim judgment against hypocrites and publicans. He demonstrated His concern for the oppressed and the shunned: the woman with the issue of blood (Luke 8:43-48), the man at the pool of Bethzatha (John 5:1-9), the Samaritan woman at the well (John 4: 7-42), the demoniacs (Matt. 8:29-33), Zacchaeus, the tax collector (Luke 19:1-10), and the lepers (Matt. 8:2-3; Luke 17:12-19).

In the first miraculous healings related in Matthew, Jesus ministered to three people on the periphery of Israelite society—a leper, a Gentile (the centurion's servant), and a woman (Peter's mother-in-law).

In Jesus' day, a woman had little identity aside from her relationship to a man. Elizabeth, for example, was called "the wife of Zechariah," and Mary, "the mother of Jesus." But Jesus often addressed women in His teaching and always in a positive way. This practice was in dramatic contrast to that of His predecessors and His contemporaries. The woman whom Jesus observed giving two coins in the temple is one example of His positive attitude toward women.

At that time, women were rarely spoken of in public. When they were mentioned, the reference was nearly always negative or demeaning. Yet Jesus included women in this male-dominated society, leaving no doubt that His message was for women as well as for men.

A dramatic example of His inclusion of women occurred when Jesus, speaking in the synagogue, described a woman as "a daughter of Abraham." Men were called "sons of Abraham." But it was unheard of to include a woman in this way. Imagine the electrifying effect Jesus' words had that day on the women who could observe but not participate in the service in any way.

Use of Scripture

As a rabbi, Jesus was thoroughly familiar with Scripture, referring to passages of the Hebrew Scripture repeatedly in His teaching. He instructed His listeners to "search the Scriptures," and told them that "they testify on my behalf " (John 5:39). He understood the power of the Word.

His teaching was filled with references to Old Testament accounts. These are only a few of many examples:

• The persecution of the prophets (Matt. 5:12)
• The judgment of Sodom and Gomorra (Matt. 10:15)

• The actions of David (Matt. 12:3)
• Jonah and Nineveh (Matt. 12:40-41)
• The blood of Abel (Matt. 23:35)
• Lot's wife (Luke 17:32)

Jesus referred to Scripture in major events in His life. As recorded in Matthew 4:1-11, when He was tempted by the Devil in the wilderness, He quoted Scripture three times, preceding each statement with "It is written."

In His first sermon in Nazareth (Luke 4:14-30), Jesus quoted the first part of Isaiah 61. When He cleansed the temple (Matt. 21:12), He quoted Isaiah 56:7: "My house shall be called a house of prayer." In foretelling His death and the desertion of the disciples, He referred to Zechariah 13: 7. And on the cross when He cried "My God, my God, why have you forsaken me?" (Mark 15:34), He was quoting Psalm 22:1.

Many other examples could be given. Jesus quoted Scripture frequently in His teaching. Other times He referred to Scriptural texts without quoting them directly. Since Scripture was well-known and respected, it provided a familiar point of reference for those who heard Him, and it lent authority to His teaching.

We as speakers, however, need to be aware that today's listeners are not as familiar with Scripture. If you tell an audience, "God will help you slay your Goliath," without telling the story, listeners may shrug their shoulders and say, "Who's this guy Goliath? And why would I want to kill him?"

Focus on Particular Interests

Jesus was very careful to use illustrations that had special appeal to those He was addressing.

He told fishermen, as He called them in the midst of their routine activities to follow Him, "From now on you will catch men." They could relate to what He was saying and, no doubt, pictured instantly the "catch" of people they could have as Jesus' disciples (Luke 5:1-11).

When speaking to tillers of the soil, He talked about seed— faith as small as a mustard seed (Matt. 13:31-32), seed falling on barren ground (Mark 4:13-20). His listeners had experienced the crop failure resulting from planting in poor soil. What He said gave them hope as they envisioned a rich harvest. They knew that a mustard seed, one of the tiniest of seeds, would grow two to six feet in height, and sometimes even nine or ten. From His illustration, Jesus' hearers comprehended that the faith He spoke of could yield unexpected results. Jesus immediately captured their attention—and gained their understanding.

Every shepherd could relate to Jesus' reference to the shepherd who enters the sheepfold through the door while the thief finds another way to enter. Every shepherd would know, too, that sheep will not follow a stranger's voice, but will follow the shepherd's voice only (John 10:1-18). Using this language, Jesus showed them the way to life through the gate, offering them life through His love as their shepherd.

Common, Familiar Examples

Jesus used illustrations about common things, things people used in their everyday lives.

In the Sermon on the Mount, He spoke of His listeners as the "salt of the earth" and then added, "but if the salt loses its flavor, how shall it be seasoned? It is then good for nothing but to be thrown out and trampled underfoot by men." His listeners knew exactly what He meant. Salt was important in their culture, for seasoning food as well as for preserving it. Eating together, for example, was referred to as "sharing salt." This reference had special meaning for those who had visited nearby Taricheae on the Sea of Galilee, the site of the great salteries where fish were prepared for market. Jesus' message, then, in calling His disciples the salt of the earth, was that they had an important mission, even as salt has a vital purpose. Yet salt can become useless if it becomes so mixed with other substances that it loses its function.

Jesus compared the kingdom of heaven to the task of making bread, a daily, time-consuming responsibility in the Jewish household. He described how the woman takes three measures of meal and mixes in the yeast, or leaven, until it thoroughly permeates every part of the dough (Matt. 13:33). The quantity of flour in Jesus' illustration would have been startling, since three measures equals about ten gallons, enough to make bread for up to 150 people. The listeners were no doubt surprised by the jarring extravagance. Jesus used a common, familiar task to make a startling new point.

He told them that a man does not put new wine into old wineskins because to do so will cause the old wineskins to burst, the wine to spill, and the wineskins to be ruined (Luke 5:37-38). His listeners had, no doubt, seen such a thing happen or were at least familiar with the fact that the process of fermentation would strain a worn leather skin to the point of splitting. They knew that using new wineskins during fermentation protected the wine as well as the skin.

Jesus warned against false prophets who would come in deceptive guises. He used fruit to illustrate the importance of carefully observing their deeds and attitudes. He said, "Every good tree bears good fruit, but a bad tree bears bad fruit. A good tree cannot bear bad fruit, nor can a bad tree bear good fruit. Every tree that does not bear good fruit is cut down and thrown into the fire. Therefore by their fruits you will know them" (Matt. 7:17-20). Although this example does clarify our understanding today, it brought even greater clarity to the original listeners. In Palestine, there was little combustible material for heating homes. Any tree that was not producing fruit was immediately chopped down to provide precious firewood for the hearth and warmth for the family.

If Jesus were speaking in person to us today, very likely He would use examples of computers, the Internet, space travel, rush-hour traffic, and the money market—subjects that are an integral part of our daily lives.

Questions

Have you ever noticed how often Jesus used questions in communicating with people? This approach was one frequently used by rabbis.

In her dissertation, Joan Lyon Gibbons places Jesus' numerous questions into eight different categories.[2] The questions she labels "a challenge to current behavior," she says, are "the most immediately personal."

Most other [question] patterns are more concerned with teaching. These questions may also have the impact of instruction, but it is because they are grounded in an immediacy of I-Thou experience....These are wonderful questions, in that their intent is not for an answer, as one would make response with a period at the end. These are questions which expect insight, leading to new action. These are questions which assume the tree of the knowledge of good and evil, planted in the garden of psyche.[3]

Examples of such questions include the following: "Are you able to drink the cup that I drink, and be baptized with the baptism that I am baptized with?" (Mark 10:39); "What? Could you not watch with Me one hour?" (Matt. 26:40); "Why are you so fearful? How is it that you have no faith?" (Mark 4:40); "Why do you also transgress the commandment of God because of your tradition?" (Matt. 15:3); and "Why does this generation seek a sign?" (Mark 8:12).

Another type of question Gibbons identifies is alternatives leading to a choice or decision. Some of Jesus' questions of this type follow: "Which is easier, to say to the paralytic, 'Your sins are forgiven you,' or to say, 'Arise, take up your bed and walk'? (Mark 2:9); "So which of these three do you think was neighbor to him who fell among the thieves?" (Luke 10:36); "Which of the two did the will of His father?" (Matt. 21:31); "Tell Me, therefore, which of them will love him more?" (Luke 7:42); and "The baptism of John — was it from heaven or from men? Answer Me" (Mark 11:30).

One of Jesus' most unusual uses of a question, related in John 21:15, occurred after Peter denied Him three times. Since Jesus was not at all shy about confronting wrongdoing, the gentleness of His question to Peter, which He posed three times, is surprising: "Simon son of John, do you love me?" Why did He ask that question? The answer has to be because He knew the question would accomplish His purpose. That simple question would have a much more dramatic and lasting effect on Peter than any amount of tongue lashing could possibly have had. The question would stop Peter in his tracks, penetrating to the very depths of his being. Peter would never deny Him again.

Jesus' use of questions provoked thought and reaction and cut to the heart of the matter — and to the heart of the hearer. The nature of questions is such that they can penetrate a person's outer defenses and arouse thinking and feeling processes, without causing the immediate rejection or defensiveness that a direct accusation often brings.

Anecdotes

Jesus was an extraordinary storyteller who used colorful anecdotes extensively to capture the imagination of His listeners. Matthew 13:34 states that "He never spoke to them without at least one illustration." In Mark 4:2 we read, "His usual method of teaching was to tell the people stories" (Living Bible).

Jesus' listeners were thoroughly familiar with this technique. Rabbis often taught in parables; hundreds of parables are found throughout the rabbinical writings known as the Talmud and the Midrash.[4] The English word "parable" is a transliteration of the Greek word *parabole*. The word's two roots come from the Greek words *para* (beside or alongside) and *ballein* (to throw). Roy B. Zuck defines a parable as "a story that places one truth beside another to clarify or emphasize a point. An unknown, unclear, or abstract idea is explained by being placed verbally along with something already known, clear, or concrete."[5]

Jesus' stories were short and to the point. One of His best known parables, the Good Samaritan, is told in only six verses in Luke 10:30-35. His stories dealt with common, everyday things and occupations familiar to everyone. They were also filled with suspense and contained an element of surprise. Most of them involved a great deal of conflict between fascinating people.

And as Zuck points out, Jesus told each of His stories for a specific purpose, "explicit or implicit, calling for decisions, appealing for action, inviting spiritual change".

> To make a judgment about him, to repent or to forgive, to be warned or comforted, to renounce pride or greed, to persist in prayer and obedience, to be compassionate and watchful, to acknowledge God's sovereignty and plans—these are some of the Lord's parabolic purposes."[6]

Several Examples to Make the Same Point

Jesus often used more than one example to make the same point. If one story didn't make His message clear, perhaps another would. Or if the listeners couldn't relate to one illustration, perhaps they could relate to another.

Jesus gave not one, but three illustrations in response to complaints from religious leaders that He was allowing tax collectors and notorious sinners to crowd around Him, listen to His sermons, and even eat with Him. He told of the man who lost one out of one hundred sheep and immediately went to look for it. When He found it, there was great rejoicing (Luke 15:3-7). His second illustration was that of the woman who lost one of ten pieces of silver and looked and looked until she found the lost piece. When she did, she called her friends and neighbors to share her joy (Luke 15:8-10). Jesus' third illustration of His attitude toward lost sinners was His story of the younger son who left His father's house and lived a life of sin and degradation. When he came to his senses and returned home repentant, his father gave a huge party to celebrate (Luke 15:11-32).

Objects

Jesus used objects people could see at the moment to get His point across. When the Samaritan woman came to the well to draw water, Jesus said, "If you only knew what a wonderful gift God has for you, and who I am, you would ask me for some living water!" He used the tangible water of Jacob's well to illustrate the abstract water of life (John 4:7-14).

Another instance of Jesus' use of visible objects is found in Matthew 21:18-22. When Jesus and His disciples passed by a fruitless fig tree, He spoke to it and said that it would never bear fruit. Soon afterward the fig tree withered and died. God, Jesus was saying, is interested in real fruit, not the external appearance of productivity.

Jesus used a coin handed to Him to teach the Pharisees and Herodians (Mark 12:13-17). The coin was a special one used to pay the "poll tax" and had on one side the emperor's wreathed head. Jesus seized the opportunity to remind His opponents what really counts: returning to God the things that belong to God.

Jesus used a towel and basin to illustrate humility to His disciples (John 13:4-17). One of His approaches that most deeply impacted His disciples, no doubt, was their partaking of the bread and cup at the Last Supper. Participating in communion continues to make a lasting sensory impression on Christians to this day.

Object Lesson or Illustrated Sermon

On more than one occasion, Jesus used a child to illustrate and dramatize His message. Once He set a child in the midst of His disciples and then took him in His arms. He then said, "Whoever welcomes one such child in my name welcomes me; and whoever welcomes me, welcomes not me but the one who sent me" (Mark 9: 36-37). With this object lesson, He dramatically illustrated the fact that God's view of greatness runs counter to the world's. Ancient attitudes toward children were different from those we know today. Children were considered to have little worth. So those people surrounding Jesus would have reacted with great surprise when He set a child in their midst.

On another occasion, when the disciples asked which of them would be greatest in the kingdom of heaven, Jesus again called a little child over and set him in the midst of them. He told his disciples that unless they were converted and became as that child, they would not even get into the kingdom of heaven. And He said that whoever humbles himself as that child will be greatest in the kingdom of heaven (Matt. 18:1-6).

Shock

The words and actions of Jesus often had a startling—even shocking—effect on those who heard and saw Him. One of His most astounding actions was His conversation with a Samaritan—and a woman at that. Both of those characteristics made her clearly off limits to any Jewish man, especially a rabbi, in light of the customs of the day.

Picture the reaction of those who heard Him say these words: "Do not think that I came to bring peace on earth. I did not come to bring peace but a sword" (Matt. 10:34). Picture the reaction of the disciples when in response to their request to send the crowds to the village so that they might eat, Jesus said, "You give them something to eat." (Matt 10:34) Picture Peter's reaction when, challenged for not paying the temple tax, Jesus commanded him, "Go to the sea, cast in a hook, and take the fish that comes up first. And when you have opened its mouth, you will find a piece of money; take that and give it to them for Me and you" (Matt. 17: 27). Again, picture Peter's reaction to Jesus' words, "I do not say to you, up to seven times, but up to seventy times seven" when Peter asked Jesus if he should forgive another member of the church seven times (Matt. 18:21).

Humor

Jesus skillfully used humor in His teaching. He was witty—a characteristic easily overlooked if we cloak Him in religiosity, failing to see the twinkle in His eye as He spoke and walked in the midst of the teeming masses. In fact, His general reputation for taking part in merriment evoked tremendous disapproval from His critics.

Although we can hardly classify Jesus as a stand-up comic, He was a master of irony and the ludicrous. As Harry Emerson Fosdick said, "He never jests as Socrates does, but He often lets the ripple of a happy breeze play over the surface of His mighty deep."[7]

Jesus apparently took to heart Proverbs 17:22: "A merry heart does good, like medicine." He chided the hypocrites who "disfigure their faces" in order to impress people when they fast. He said their "sad countenances" were their reward. In other words, others had already seen their sad countenances (Matt. 6:16).

Consider Jesus' description of the Pharisee's preparation for drinking (Matt. 23:25-26). The Pharisee had no intention of drinking from a cup that was not immaculately clean, or at least had the outward appearance of cleanliness. We see the Pharisee as he took great care to scrub and polish the outside of the cup. It was bright and shiny, as everyone could see. The problem was that inside there was a big mess.

What was the Pharisee going to drink? He was fastidious to ensure that there was not a gnat or other form of contamination in the water. Often, during Jesus' time, a cloth was placed over the water vessel to keep it free of dust or mosquitoes on its morning journey from the town well. But, while he went through the elaborate process of straining his drink so that not even a gnat got in, he overlooked the camel sitting inside his filthy cup. We are treated to a delightfully absurd mental picture of the Pharisee drinking from the camel-infested cup. Terrot Glover helps us imagine the hilarious scene.

> The long hairy neck slid down the throat of the Pharisee—all that amplitude of loose-hung anatomy—the hump—two humps—both of them slid down—and he never noticed—and the legs—all of them—with the whole outfit of knees and big padded feet. The

Pharisee swallowed a camel and never noticed it. It is the mixture of sheer realism with absurdity that makes the irony and gives it its force. Did no one smile as the story was told? Did no one see the scene pictured with his own mind's eye—no one grasp the humor and the irony with delight? Could any one, on the other hand, forget it? A modern teacher would have said, in our jargon, that the Pharisee had no sense of proportion—and no one would have thought the remark worth remembering.[8]

And then there's the grotesque imagery of the seventh chapter of Matthew. Jesus talked about the mote you notice in your brother's eye, while you walk around with a beam sticking out of your own eye. If you personalize this example in your own life and imagine trying to get into your car to drive home at rush hour, work at your computer, or go through a revolving door, all the while sporting a steel building beam in one eye, Jesus' example could turn into the material for a sitcom scenario.

A classic example of Jesus' use of irony is His reference to Simon as "Peter," which means "rock," (Aramaic, *cepha*; Greek, *petros*) (Matt. 16:18). At that time, Simon was anything but stable. Simon was later referred to by Jesus as a "stumbling rock" (Matt. 16:23). Soon afterward, Simon rejected Jesus' teaching and rebuked Him. He demonstrated his un-rock-like character even more dramatically by denying Jesus on three different occasions. At the time, the comparison was absurd; calling Simon a rock was similar to calling a mountain of a man "Tiny". Fortunately, Jesus' use of the word "Peter," ridiculous as it was at the time, described the man that Simon later became.

Jesus used humor skillfully to unmask hypocrisy and to make truth more palatable. As Elton Trueblood wrote, "Humor is redemptive when it leads to comic self-discovery. Christ brings such self-discovery to men who will listen and who know that they are responsible for what they hear."[9] Trueblood further noted that "God's laughter comes only with an underlying interest in our welfare. The laughter is directed at our frailties, but its purpose is to heal."[10]

Practical Approach

Jesus' message was consistently down-to-earth, applicable to the lives of those who heard His words. His was no abstract, theoretical discussion. His goal was not to establish a reputation as a great philosopher of the day, but rather to call those who heard His words to follow him. His challenge was to the heart as well as to the head.

The Impact

What effect did Jesus have on those who heard Him speak? For the answer, let's look at some texts from Scripture.

Mark 8:2 records that a multitude had been listening to Him teach for three days and had gone without food that long in order to hear Him. Again, the book of Mark records that "the common people heard him gladly" (12:37). Jesus' hearers, Luke writes, "were amazed at His teaching, for His word was with authority and ability and weight and power" (4:32 Amplified). Even the temple police said, "No man ever spoke like this Man" (John 7:46).

His message changed the lives of those who heard Him. And after more than 2,000 years, it is still changing the lives of men and women. What speaker would not like to have that kind of impact? Certainly we would all do well to study and follow the myriad imaginative approaches Jesus used to command attention and plant seeds of faith in His hearers' hearts and lives.

Chapter 2

MAKING FRIENDS WITH YOUR WORST ENEMY—YOU!

*So we may boldly say: "The Lord is my helper; I will not fear.
What can man do to me?" (Hebrews 13:6).*

Huh? What Did You Say?

D o you suffer from logophobia or embolalia? No, they're not diseases. But they can make your speech turn limpid and pale. Logophobia is the fear of speaking—a much more dignified-sounding malady than stage fright, don't you think? Embolalia is the word for speech fillers such as "y'know" "er" "um" "o.k" "right?" Y'know what I mean? Never fear. Anaphora and videocybernetics can help you out as a speaker.

Anaphora—the repetition of a word or phrase at the beginning of successive sentences or paragraphs—is the hallmark of such stirring oratory as Martin Luther King's "I Have a Dream" and John F. Kennedy's "Let Them Come to Berlin." And videocybernetics—training and coaching with video feedback—is a powerful tool for improving your skills as a speaker.

Making Peace with the Face in Your Mirror

Consider: The comic strip character Pogo waxed philosophical when he said, "We have met the enemy, and it is us."[1] Although his words of wisdom could easily apply to many areas of living, certainly one of the most appropriate applications would be to the challenging task of speaking before an audience. There is no doubt that the worst enemy most of us have as public speakers is ourselves.

There are many skills to conquer in becoming an effective speaker, but probably the biggest conquest that has to be made is that of the person we see in the mirror each morning. "Public Speaking and Other Coronary Threats" was the title used for an article by Max D. Isaacson, vice president of Maxmillan Oil Company.[2] Although it is an amusing title, most people find getting up before an audience anything but a laughing matter.

In fact, speaking before a group was listed as the number-one fear of U.S. inhabitants who ranked fourteen common fears. Fear of death was number seven on the list.[3] From this poll, we can conclude that most people would rather die than face an audience to speak.

Someone has said, "When it comes to public speaking, many are called, but few want to get up." And most of us can relate to this observation: "The brain is a remarkable thing. It starts to function the instant you are born and doesn't stop until the moment you get up to speak."[4]

"All the world's a stage," wrote Shakespeare, who might well have added, "and every player on it has stage fright." A marvelous story about stage fright involves an incident that supposedly took place in the days of the Roman Empire. It seems that a Christian was thrown to a hungry lion in the Coliseum. As the spectators cheered, the wild beast pounced. But when the Christian whispered something in the lion's ear, the beast backed away in terror. After this performance had been repeated several times, the emperor sent a centurion to find out what magic spell was making the ferocious lion cower in fear. A few minutes later the guard returned and said, "The Christian whispers in the lion's ear, 'After dinner you'll be required to say a few words.'"[5]

Remember the words of E. Hubbard: "The greatest mistake you can make in life is to be continually fearing you will make one."[6] So, although getting up in front of an audience is definitely a high-risk, stressful situation, speaking effectively and moving and influencing listeners is definitely one of the most exhilarating and satisfying adventures a person can undertake.

Coping with Stage Fright

Consider: Everyone has the problem of learning to handle nervousness, the jitters, stage fright—whatever you want to call it. Everyone gets butterflies in the stomach. The trick is to train them to fly in formation.

Even seasoned speakers and performers admit to nervousness. Theatrical immortal Otis Skinner comforted his daughter Cornelia with this insight: "I have been in the theater for 50 years, and I've never outgrown it. Any actor who claims he is immune to stage fright is either lying, or else he's no actor."[7]

So although stage fright isn't funny, it is normal, natural, and, believe it or not, even helpful—once you learn to use it to your advantage instead of your destruction. In fact, if you ever get over that feeling of nervousness as a speaker, you'll probably be one of two things—dead or lousy.

What we experience when we have stage fright is the same fight-or-flight syndrome the caveman experienced when he found himself confronted with a life-or-death situation. Picture this scenario. The caveman is strolling through the woods carrying his trusty club over his shoulder. Suddenly he hears the roar of a tiger. His body tenses; all his senses focus; his mind races. He has to make a decision, and fast! Is the tiger far enough away so that he can run for it? Or is he going to have to fight for his life and hope he can survive? Either way, some amazing changes take place in his body to equip him to carry out this incredibly stressful decision.

Adrenaline is released as a result of the physical and emotional stress, causing enormous activity throughout his body. His heart beats faster. His respiratory rate increases, resulting in more shallow breathing. More oxygen is pumped to all tissues. His mental activity speeds up significantly. And his muscle strength becomes much greater, enabling him to run faster and become closer to a match for the tiger.

The same thing happens to our bodies when we get stage fright. Well, it might be considered inappropriate to flee from the dais, and it certainly would be rude to punch out the person who just introduced you. The best solution is to learn to capitalize on the positive and eliminate the negative impacts on your transformed body.

Consider the advantages:

One advantage of stage fight is more oxygen to the brain, resulting in increased mental activity. Certainly, as speakers we need all the brain power we can get. Another advantage is increased muscle strength. Public speaking requires a lot of energy. That extra power really comes in handy.

An example of increased strength in a tense situation took place a few years ago when a woman came upon the scene of an accident near Beaumont, Texas. A child was pinned under the wheel of a truck. The driver was injured, and there was no one else in sight. The woman jumped out of her car, ran to the truck and lifted the truck enough to free the child. Later, after the child and the driver had been taken to the hospital, the woman could not budge the truck. Only the extreme stress of seeing a child under the truck's wheel activated the superhuman strength she needed.

One effect of stage fright, however, a more rapid respiratory rate, is not an asset. Shallow breathing may leave you stranded in the middle of a phrase or even a long word. Shallow breathing also results in less support for the voice. Have you ever been speaking when suddenly your voice goes out of control, sounding perhaps an octave higher?

And, of course, the increased mental activity must be ordered, not allowed to race off in all directions at once.

The good news is that the shakes, the hot and cold flashes, the nausea, the damp palms, the cold sweat dripping down the ribs, the dry throat, and the inability to focus your thinking can all be controlled.

It's exciting to know that once we learn to use our souped-up bodies to advantage, we can do a better job than we normally could. We can capitalize on the increased energy. Our brains will be sharper, our thinking clearer. And there are definite steps we can take to cope with any negative changes brought about when our bodies get ready to fight or flee.

Fifteen Ways to Overcome Stage Fright

1. A powerful way to tame those butterflies is to pray and to quote Scripture, aloud, to yourself. As Christian speakers, we don't have to do it on our own. As in all things, God is able to provide the help and encouragement we need. Try saying aloud five times, "I can do all things through Christ who strengthens me" (Phil 4:13). Note the calmness and empowerment this truth brings to your mind, body, and emotions.

2. Dress comfortably in clothes you like and feel good in. It's important to you psychologically to feel confident about the way you look. As someone said, "You can't lead a cavalry

charge if you think you look funny sitting on a horse."[8] You need to think you look like a seasoned speaker.

3. Be well prepared. Don't wait until the last minute to put your speech together. Rehearse several times. Program your mind with your material to the point that you can give your speech regardless of what might happen.

4. Concentrate on your message. When you believe you have something important to share with your audience, it's easy to get excited about what you're going to tell them. When you focus on your message, you likely will forget about yourself. As Lady Bird Johnson observed, "The way you overcome shyness is to become so wrapped up in something, you forget to be afraid."[9]

5. Take several deep breaths. The increased respiratory rate we usually experience as a result of stage fright can cause lots of problems. Not only do we run out of breath every few words; we also lack the support necessary for good vocal production. Breathing deeply breaks this cycle and has a calming effect. A good approach is to breathe from the diaphragm. Breathe in on a count of four, hold your breath four counts, and breathe out on the word "easy." This breathing can be done unobtrusively, even if you are seated in front of a crowd of people.

6. Move around. Movement releases nervous energy and restores a feeling of calmness. If you are waiting in the wings to go on, take some large, brisk steps, and flail your arms around. If you're seated on the dais, of course, you can't move that much, but you can take advantage of your walk to the speaker's stand. And what if suddenly you start getting nervous in the middle of your speech? Find an excuse to make large gestures, move away from the lectern, and sip a glass of water (a perfectly acceptable thing for a speaker to do). If you're trapped at the speaker's stand by a mike you can't move, ask a rhetorical question and move while you're giving the audience time to think of the answer.

7. Picture yourself doing well. Use positive mental imaging. See yourself in your mind's eye being introduced, walking

to the speaker's stand, speaking to a warm, responsive audience. See how well you're doing. Hear your words flowing without hesitation. Experience the laughter of the audience, the enthusiastic applause after you are finished. See yourself as successful and run several replays of your success. Many top athletes use this positive mental imaging technique and swear by its effectiveness.

Consider an amazing example. U. S. Army Major Nesmith was confined for seven years as a prisoner during the Vietnam War. His "cell" was a small cage, approximately four-and-one half feet tall and slightly over five feet long, in which he was unable to stretch out to his full length. The first few months he did virtually nothing but pray, hope for his release, and harbor deep resentment toward his captors. But he realized he had to take definite, positive steps if he were to retain his sanity and stay alive. An avid but average golfer who shot in the nineties, he decided to play golf mentally in his cage. He selected his favorite golf course and "played" a full round of eighteen holes, every day, down to the last detail. He saw the beautiful trees, felt the gentle breeze and the sunshine, smelled the freshly cut grass on the course, and listened to the birds chirping. He saw himself hitting the ball accurately with a correct swing and saw it flying down the center of the fairway and onto the green to the exact spot he had selected. It took him the same four hours to play his golf game mentally as it had when he had actually played on that golf course. He went through this same exercise seven days a week for seven years.

When he was released and returned home, one of the first things he wanted to do was play a round of golf on the course he had envisioned. To his utter amazement, he shot an impressive seventy-four. Even though he had not played in seven years and his physical condition had deteriorated, mental imaging had helped him to improve his actual performance.[10]

8. Make no negative confession. Whatever you do, don't say, "I know I'm going to blow it," or "I'm so nervous, I'll never get through this speech." Thinking that way is bad enough, but there's something about saying negative things that feeds your fears and makes them turn into horrible monsters. Instead, make

that negative a positive by telling yourself that you are going to do the best you've ever done. For the public speaker, death and life really are in the power of the tongue (Prov. 18:21).

9. Gain confidence by doing. Practice makes perfect. Speaking is a skill, and, like any other skill, requires continued effort and experience. Success builds on success.

If you feel inadequate in expressing yourself effectively, you're in good company. Moses certainly was a reluctant speaker. Remember what he said? "O my Lord, I am not eloquent, neither before nor since You have spoken to Your servant; but I am slow of speech and slow of tongue. So the Lord said to him, "Who has made man's mouth? Have not I, the Lord? Now therefore, go, and I will be with your mouth and teach you what you shall say" (Exodus 4:10-12).

In spite of God's assurances, Moses continued to protest and profess his inadequacies. He finally begged God into letting Aaron be his spokesman. In case God does not have an Aaron waiting in the wings for you and you still feel inadequate, consider these speakers who did not have everything going for them and yet made a tremendous impact.

John F. Kennedy had a heavy New England accent. Eleanor Roosevelt's voice was not the most pleasant by anyone's standard. Dwight D. Eisenhower spoke in a halting monotone. Still their words swayed millions.

10. Remember your audience is made up of people just like you. They want you to do well. Unless you saw them come in with a basket of rotten tomatoes, you can assume that they really are on your side. They don't want their time wasted by a lousy, boring speaker. An ill-at-ease speaker makes the listener ill-at-ease and embarrassed, too.

11. Remember an occasion when you did a really terrific job as a speaker, and relive it—several times. Most of us do just the opposite. We think of a dismal experience of failure such as a time in third grade when we gave a book report, forgot what we were going to say next, and ran crying from the room. We need to remove those negative tapes from our mental library and focus on the positive ones.

12. Come to terms with the fact that if you are going to be a speaker, you are going to make mistakes. That is, unless you consistently type 180 words a minute without an error or hit a home run with every swing of the bat. A mistake need not be fatal. If you learn to laugh it off and let your audience enjoy it with you instead of becoming embarrassed, your mistake can even become a bridge to better rapport.

13. Pick out friendly faces and make eye contact with them. An encouraging expression on a listener's face can do wonders to promote confidence. Avoid looking at someone who has folded arms, a crabby look, or fidgety movements.

14. Cooperate with your body. Cooperation includes getting enough rest the night before so your energy will be at a high level. It also means eating sensibly. Having a huge meal just before speaking is asking for problems. Although the effect of different foods varies with the individual, most speakers would do well to avoid sugar-laden foods, too much caffeine, and all alcoholic beverages. For most people, a smaller-than-usual meal of high protein foods is a safe bet.

15. Last, but certainly not least, do a relaxation exercise. There are several to choose from, but one that you can do even while you're seated on the platform is the Spaghetti Exercise. Just be sure you don't get so relaxed you fall off your chair.

The Spaghetti Exercise: Picture yourself as a piece of uncooked spaghetti that is slowly dropped, feet first, in boiling water. Feel your toes get soft, your feet, your ankles, the calves of your legs, all the way up to the top of your head.

Body Relaxation: Dr. Boino Kiveloff of the New York Infirmary and Beekman Downtown Hospital has developed a daily exercise to help keep one's blood pressure at a healthy level.[11] He recommends doing the exercise three times daily, but it can help a speaker right before a speaking engagement also.

Steal away to a quiet corner, a restroom, or wherever you can be alone for a few minutes.

1. Stand in a comfortable position with your arms hanging loosely at your sides. Relax your elbows and knees, keeping your hands unclenched.
2. Tighten every muscle in your body, either in unison or by groups. Still tensed, breathe normally and count aloud to six.
3. Relax your muscles and rest briefly.
4. Repeat the exercise two more times.

Progressive Relaxation Exercise: The sixteen steps in this exercise require you to tense each muscle group for six seconds, then completely relax them for thirty seconds.

Muscle Groups

1. Dominant hand
2. Dominant upper arm
3. Non-dominant hand
4. Non-dominant upper arm
5. Forehead
6. Eyes and nose
7. Mouth and jaw
8. Neck and throat
9. Upper back
10. Stomach
11. Dominant upper leg
12. Dominant lower leg
13. Dominant foot
14. Non-dominant upper leg
15. Non-dominant lower leg
16. Non-dominant foot

Other Relaxation Exercises:

1. Upper arm: Press your elbow down and pull toward your body for six seconds, then relax 30 seconds.
2. Forehead: Wrinkle your brow into a frown. Relax.
3. Mouth and jaw: Clench your jaw. Relax.
4. Neck and throat: Press your head back against the chair. Relax.
5. Upper back: Pull your shoulder ups and forward. Relax.
6. Stomach: Pull your stomach in as far as you can. Relax. Push your stomach out as far as you can. Relax.
7. Upper leg: Lift your leg slightly. Relax.
8. Lower leg: Point your toes away from your head. Relax.

"I'm Sorry. In Fact, I'm the Sorriest..."

Consider: When tempted to apologize, don't! If you're a flop as a speaker, the audience will find out soon enough. Besides, if you don't tell them, they may never know.

Think about the reactions to these types of apologies from a speaker.

"Please forgive me. I'm really nervous."

1. Listener's reaction: "He does look nervous. Even his hands are shaking. Boy, is he ever making me uncomfortable."

2. Speaker's reaction: "Oh, my goodness. I'm even more nervous than I thought I was."

"I'm really sorry, but I just didn't have time to prepare this speech the way I really wanted to."

1. Listener's reaction: "Thanks a lot for wasting my valuable time. Ho hum!"

2. Speaker's reaction: "This is really going to be a bummer. Why didn't I work on this instead of watching that movie? I'll just have to fumble through."

"I don't know why I was asked to speak on this subject. There are a lot of people who know more about it than I do."

1. Listener's reaction: "I don't know either. Is this ever going to be awful…one long bore."

2. Speaker's reaction: "I really feel inadequate and unsure of myself."

"I'm really not much of a speaker."

1. Listener's reaction: "Well, that's obvious without saying."

2. Speaker's reaction: "I just hope I can make it through this."

As a speaker, remove the word "sorry" from your vocabulary… except in a couple of instances.

1. If you are unavoidably late and keep the audience waiting, you owe them an apology and an explanation.

2. If the audience is uncomfortable, and the problem cannot be corrected, you need to express concern for their comfort and well-being.

But what if something happens you just can't ignore? Say, for example, you are walking to the lectern or the pulpit with great poise and confidence, trip over a cord and fall flat on your face. What do you do then?

Rather than getting embarrassed, turn the incident into an asset by getting your audience to laugh with you. You can say something like this: "Well, my speech teacher told me to get the audience's attention, but this is ridiculous." Or "My pastor said I should be humble, but maybe I carried it a little too far this time." Let the audience know it's o.k. to laugh. Otherwise, they'll be embarrassed for themselves and for you.

Yield not to the temptation to apologize. You'll be sorry if you do!

Keep on Keeping on

Consider: There's an old Spanish saying: "Ay Jalisco! No te rajes!" Although something is lost in the translation, this rallying cry basically, means: "Don't give up. Keep on keeping on!"

This expression would make a great motto for all of us who are trying to master the fine art of public speaking. No one is born a good speaker. Public speaking is a skill. And, like any other skill, to be mastered it must be practiced correctly until it becomes second nature. You will eventually forget about the mechanics and just do it.

Between beginning to speak and mastering public speaking, you must expect to go through a learning process that is sometimes painful and discouraging. After all, how many times did you fall down before you learned to walk? Did you get the basketball in the hoop the first time you tried? Did you cook a gourmet meal the first time you stepped into the kitchen? Every skill requires time, effort, practice, and persistence.

A reporter said to George Bernard Shaw one day, "You have a marvelous gift for oratory. How did you develop it?" Shaw replied, "I learned to speak as men learn to skate or cycle—by doggedly making a fool of myself until I got used to it."[12]

As Ralph Waldo Emerson pointed out, "All the great speakers were bad speakers at first."[13]

After a brilliant piano concert capped by thunderous applause, the Queen of England said to the artist, "Mr. Paderewski, you are a genius." Bowing gravely, Paderewski replied, "Before I became a genius, your Majesty, I was a drudge."[14]

All of us have to be drudges—to risk failure—before we can become geniuses. But remember, you never fail until you stop trying.

If you still aren't convinced you can become an excellent public speaker, consider the equipment this speaker possessed:

- He had a congenital lisp and stammer.
- His voice lacked the rich resonance associated with a successful platform speaker.
- His five-foot hunched frame was hardly an imposing presence.
- He fainted dead away when he first spoke in the British Parliament.

And yet he became recognized as one of the most eloquent orators of the twentieth century. His words changed the course of history.

Even though Winston Churchill had little going for him, "in his command of the English language, he commanded the destiny of free men. Through his mastery of the tongue, he rose in Parliament to prime minister and eventually saved the West."[15] Churchill knew that if he were going to accomplish what he felt compelled to do, he would have to overcome his limitations and fears and become a good speaker.

As Christian speakers, can we be content to do any less? Especially when we can rest assured that the Lord will be with our mouths and teach us what we are to say (Exod. 4:12).

Chapter 3

PRESENTING YOURSELF AS A SPEAKER

For I will give you a mouth and wisdom which all of your
adversaries will not be able to contradict or resist (Luke 21:15).

Consider: In the first four minutes, the speaker is either received or rejected by the audience. We gather information…

- 87% by sight
- 7% by hearing
- 3½% by smell
- 1½% by touch
- 1% by taste

So what your audience sees is vitally important. Listeners need visual stimulation, a point of activity to focus on. Gestures, body language, appearance, eye contact, posture and facial animation, in addition to other visual stimuli, are vitally important.

The average person speaks about 125 words per minute. The average person thinks at a rate nearly four times faster.[1] We say that our minds wander, but actually they gallop ahead of the speaker like a runaway race horse. Speakers have to do everything possible to rivet the listeners' attention.

Because of TV, the average person's attention span is now said to be only about seven minutes. Then it's time for the commercial and a chance to run to the fridge for a snack or put the clothes in the dryer. A speaker needs a variety of pace and activity to overcome the distractions of the avid television viewer. These facts point up the importance of making sure your listeners' eyes have pleasant, positive stimuli to keep them interested enough to listen to your message.

Appearance

Consider: How you look initially determines how willing people will be to listen to you.

As a speaker, think of yourself as a visual. That's what you become when you appear before an audience. Your manner of dress and attention to small details of grooming make an indelible impression about your message and the organization you represent... before you ever open your mouth.

These are some important areas to keep in mind.

Simplicity should be the keynote. Solid colors are safest. Any patterns should be small and subdued. Bold patterns can be distracting, even dizzying—especially in the case of a speaker who moves around a great deal.

The colors you choose have an impact. If you want to project power and authority, dress in dark colors, preferably black or navy. Very bright colors stimulate an audience.

Formality in dress should match the top level of your audience, or be one notch above. A certain level of formality in dress projects authority and credibility as a speaker. However, if the formality is overdone, an audience may feel somewhat intimidated. Also, a negative effect can result if a speaker is really overdressed for the occasion. Consider, for instance, an executive who shows up in a three-piece suit to speak at a lake retreat where everyone is wearing jeans or for a hard-hat crew of construction workers.

Comfort in dress is important. A speaking engagement is not the occasion to break in a new pair of shoes, regardless of how stunning they might look. Cramped, aching feet usually result eventually in a pained expression on the face. Clothing should be unrestrictive and should permit absolute freedom of movement. This consideration is especially important in relation to making gestures.

Dress for confidence. Wear something you really like in which you feel that you look your very best. Although a new outfit often gives a person a psychological lift, you are probably safer to select something you're used to and that feels a part of you. At least give a new wardrobe piece a trial run to be sure everything works and fits properly before wearing it on the podium.

Wear slightly lighter-weight clothing than you normally would. Public speaking is hard work and usually results in a rise in body temperature. You may also want to consider dressing in layers, so that you have a removable outer garment.

Be sure the clothes you select will remain as crisp-looking for your speech as they were when you left for your speaking engagement. Some fabrics, such as linen, simply wrinkle more easily than others.

Avoid dangling or large pieces of jewelry. Not only can they be distracting; they can also be very tempting for the speaker to play with—which is even more distracting.

Don't wear anything you might unconsciously fiddle with—for example, a loose-fitting ring. Also, don't have anything on the speaker's stand that you might be tempted to play with. Clicking a retractable pen repeatedly, for instance, can be a major interference for your audience.

If you wear glasses, for goodness's sake, keep them on instead of jerking them off and thrusting them back on. If you are in a brightly lighted area, you should probably spray your glasses with an anti-glare spray (available in photography shops).

Women have more options in dress—and more pitfalls. Very high heels can be tricky since they tend to throw a speaker off balance and make smooth, natural movement more difficult. Straight skirts are also risky, especially for the woman who will be seated on the platform before being introduced. A good idea is to sit in a chair and have someone check out just how much you will be revealing from the audience's perspective.

Clanking bracelets and shiny jewelry should be avoided. Hair styles that hide part of the face or that allow strands of hair to fall down over the face are also risky. Beware of wearing a tight girdle. It makes correct breathing difficult indeed. Taking along an extra pair of hose is a good insurance policy in case of a last-minute run.

But men have their snares, too. Special attention should be given to the fit of the coat through the shoulders to be sure arms are free to move comfortably and without restriction. A precautionary measure for men is to empty jacket and pant pockets before ascending the podium. Many a speech has been ruined by a speaker's clanging his change or keys in his pocket...nearly always without even realizing he's doing it.

Simplicity in dress is a good rule of thumb. Wearing something that is too flashy or high fashion may look smashing, but it also may move the spotlight away from what you're saying onto what you're wearing. After all, you want your audience to remember your words—not your outfit.

Posture

Consider: A public speaker should appear "bigger than life." This posture has to do with bearing, taking space, stage presence, and an inner mindset.

Try the "Exercise of the Big and the Little" to get a real feel for the way your thinking about yourself can transform your outward appearance and your self-confidence. This exercise can be fun to do with another person or in a small group with each person going through the routine.

Take a few minutes to tell yourself that you are very small physically, that you're insignificant, not worth a flip, that no one would be interested in anything you might have to say. After playing that mind game, walk across the room trying to be as tiny and unnoticed as possible.

Next, tell yourself that physically you are of gigantic proportions. You also are the most important person in the whole world, whom everyone loves and admires, and everyone wants to hear every word you utter. When you're all psyched up, walk across the room as the largest, most valuable person in the world.

Check out the difference a modified way of thinking made for you. In a group, talk about the appearance of each person projecting the two different personas. Your mindset about yourself makes a significant impact on your confidence and the way you are perceived by others.

The great Greek orator Demosthenes worked very hard to overcome his limitations as a speaker. One of his problems was his posture. To improve his bearing before an audience, he practiced speaking before a mirror with two swords hanging from the ceiling. The point of each sword barely touched his shoulders, so that if he made any awkward movement, he would stab himself.[2] Although this practice is not necessarily recommended as a rehearsal technique, it does illustrate the importance of posture to a man with a centuries-long reputation as an outstanding speaker.

Slouching presents a sloppy appearance, whereas erect posture projects authority and confidence.

Members of an audience will size you up from the moment they see you and decide—at least subconsciously—if you're going to be worth hearing.

Stage Presence

Of course, the way you are dressed and stand makes a statement, but another vital part of the message the audience receives about you is determined by your stage presence. The following tips are important points to keep in mind.

If you are seated on the platform before you speak, be aware that you are being watched and graded as a speaker before you ever begin.

Lounging in your chair or staring off into space gives a sloppy impression. Sitting up straight with an interested, involved-looking expression in all that's happening makes an initial good impression.

Also, beware of gripping the arms of your chair, wringing your hands, or making repetitive movements with your feet. These are tip-offs to nervousness and should be avoided.

Men should sit with both feet flat on the floor. Crossing one leg over the other usually results in doing strange things with your feet, such as moving in a circular or swinging motion. This not only distracts the audience from the speaker before you; it also makes a statement: "You are nervous!"

The safest thing for a woman is to sit with feet crossed at the ankle. This makes a more attractive line under a skirt and also helps keep the skirt down in front.

The way you get up from your chair is important also. Use your leg muscles to lift you quickly. More or less unfolding out of your chair looks sloppy and unenthusiastic.

Walk rapidly and with good posture and verve to the speaker's stand as if you can hardly wait to share your thoughts, smiling and making eye contact with the audience as you go. It's important to take space by showing outward confidence even before you utter the first word. The audience needs to know you are in command. Never start speaking before you get to the speaker's stand.

Once there say "thank you" to the person who introduced you. Pause and make eye contact with people in different sections of the audience. Give your audience time to get used to seeing you there. Then begin your remarks.

During the speech, your feet should be apart, approximately at shoulder width. Weight should be equally distributed. Putting your weight on one foot throws your shoulders out of line and makes you as a speaker resemble the Leaning Tower of Pisa. It also leads to shifting your weight to the other foot, and then back and forth, until you look like a rocking horse.

The head should be up so that the face, and especially the eyes, can be easily seen. Know your material so well that you only have to glance at your notes instead of keeping your eyes fixed on them for long periods of time.

Remember that the lectern is there to hold your notes; it is not for use as a reclining couch. Although resting your hands occasionally on the speaker's stand is acceptable, clutching it or leaning on it is strictly taboo.

Arms should be away from the body, not glued to your side like a tin soldier's. An old English theatrical expression goes thus: "Let your armpits breathe."

When using a microphone, be sure that it is adjusted to the proper level for your height. It should not cover your face or be positioned so that you cannot maintain solid, straight, and square posture. Don't play with the mike stand or cord.

Beware of distracting unconscious habits such as smoothing your hair, touching your nose, scratching, pulling on hair or clothing, or playing with a pen or pencil. Ask a friend in the audience to note such behavior and report to you later, since many of those kinds of repetitive movements go unnoticed by the perpetrator.

Once you've finished, leave the speaker's stand with as much aplomb as you approached it. Shrugging your shoulders, showing disgust with yourself, or acting as though you're glad that's over can ruin an otherwise effective presentation.

Gestures

Consider: The fact that people respond fifty-five percent to your body language and expression, thirty-seven percent to your vocal inflection and only eight percent to what you say makes a rather startling statement about the importance of gestures.[3]

Hands? What to do with them? One seasoned speaker said, "My biggest problem as a novice speaker was knowing what to do with those things hanging at the ends of my arms. All of a sudden it seemed as though they weighed at least fifty pounds each. No matter what I did with them, they seemed awkward and in the way. It took a bunch of speeches before I was able to turn my hands into assets instead of liabilities."

Few things about speaking can have a more positive or a more negative effect on the overall impact of the presentation than the use of gestures. Shakespeare says in *The Winter's Tale*, "There was speech in their dumbness, language in their very gesture."

There are three main benefits of gestures when they are used to advantage.

1. They can emphasize the main points of your presentation.

2. Appropriate gestures allow your audience to better follow your train of thought.

3. Gestures may be used to involve your audience in what you're saying.

Let's discuss some roles not to play as a speaker.

The Jeweler	plays with ring, watch, bracelet.
The Prayer	folds hands in front of body; looks as though he's praying to just make it through.
The Stern Parent	stands with arms crossed over the chest.
The Key Executive	fiddles with keys, coins, and other wonderful things found in pockets.
The Fig Leaf	stands with hands folded in front—looking much as Adam must have looked in his first outfit.
The Soldier at Parade Rest	holds hands behind back.
Dishpan Hands	conceals hands in pockets so no one can see them.
The Athletic Type	demonstrates athletic prowess with a running series of jabs, punches, uppercuts, and karate chops.[4]

Most speakers who play those roles get locked into position until the audience suspects rigor mortis has set in.

The antidote to being a rigid Robert or Ruth is to start with your arms held loosely by your sides, keeping space between your arms and your body. Don't hold them too close or you'll look stiff, as if your arms are glued down. With your arms by your side, you are ready to move them freely at your instant bidding.

The size of the gestures you use should be tailored to the size of the area in which you're speaking and the number of people in the audience. A good rule of thumb is this: Use very broad gestures in a huge hall, but pare them down in a more intimate setting.

Appropriate gestures can go a long way toward making your presentation more interesting and dramatic, keeping your audience's attention, and reinforcing what you're saying. But don't let gestures take precedence over your message. Remember, if the listener is paying more attention to what your arms and hands are doing than to what you're saying, you're being upstaged!

Using Gestures Effectively

In *Hamlet*, Shakespeare referred to gestures when he said, "Do not saw the air," and "Fit the action to the word and the word to the action."

Here are some other suggestions for using gestures well:

- Gestures should be, or appear to be, spontaneous.
- The whole body should be involved, not just a hand or a part of your arm.
- Gestures should be broad and sweeping with arms away from the body. Gestures with the upper arm held rigidly against the body look awkward, even grotesque. Move arms and hands from in front of your body out to the sides.
- Remember that using the exact same gesture over and over gets monotonous.
- Avoid the self-touching movements, covering your mouth, playing with the mike or pointer, gripping the podium, or wringing your hands. Your gestures and facial expressions should be a matching pair. For example, if you're talking about something frightening, have a fearful expression with your arm up as if protecting yourself.

- Practice making very large, exaggerated gestures. A good exercise is to say phrases such as "way up there," or "look over there" as you sweep your arm in front of you from your side, as high as you can reach in an exaggerated manner. Once you get used to the feel of doing a gesture so broadly that it looks grotesque, you can tame it down to an appropriate size, and it will feel natural and comfortable.

- Practice in front of a mirror or, better yet, with a video recorder to see how your movements look.

- Be sure your body language isn't sending a message you don't want to give. For example, covering your mouth can tell your audience you're not sure of what you're saying, or may even give the impression that you're not telling the truth.

- Remember that a speaker's stand forms a barrier between your audience and you. Stepping out from behind the stand can be very effective, especially when you want to seem more intimate in a certain part of your speech or when you are telling an anecdote that can be dramatized. If you can speak without notes, so much the better—don't use a lectern at all. If you are a frequent speaker, you might consider purchasing your own lectern made of plastic or Lucite, allowing your audience to see all of you at all times. If you are unusually short, take along a platform. Otherwise, you will appear child-like behind a huge speaker's stand.

- Although moving around when speaking is good, be sure that movement is with purpose. Repetitious movement, such as pacing, can become monotonous and distracting.

Eye Contact

Consider: Eye contact forms a very personal bond with another person. It's an absolute essential for establishing good rapport with an audience.

Someone who will not look at them when they're carrying on a conversation irritates most people. Looking down and glancing around gives the impression of untrustworthiness. Staring off in space says, "I'm bored" or "I'm not interested." We want to talk with someone who will look at us—both when we're talking and when he's talking. The same is true of talking with someone in an audience.

The eye—probably more than any other part of the body—gives us a glimpse into the mind of the other person. It's interesting to note that it can give us definite cues as to how what we're saying is being received. If the pupil is being enlarged, we know that the listener is reacting positively to what we are saying.

There are several benefits to maintaining eye contact with your audience.

1. You give the impression that you are truly interested in the listeners when you look them in the eye and maintain that contact for several seconds. The major benefit is that you can establish rapport quickly and easily.

2. Looking at someone without hesitancy projects confidence, power, and authority. It also conveys openness and honesty.

3. Eye contact involves the audience and helps keep them interested in what you're saying.

Here are some points to remember about eye contact.

- Eye contact with your audience should begin the moment you are introduced as a speaker—as you rise and walk to the speaker's stand.

- After saying "thank you" to the person who introduced you, you should pause and make eye contact with people in several sections of your audience. The audience needs that time to look at you and get ready to listen. This practice also shows confidence and helps you to "take charge."

- Eye contact in the beginning of your remarks is extremely important as you make that vital first impression as a speaker. Your opening remarks should be committed to memory so that you are free to look at the audience without distraction.

- In order to establish solid eye contact, look at a person from three to five seconds. This type of eye contact gives the listeners the impression that you are speaking just to them and makes your remarks seem personal.

- Glancing at a person for only a second and then changing to someone else makes a speaker look shifty and lessens the audience's confidence in what you have to say. An excellent example of the adverse effect of darting-eye glances is the Nixon-Kennedy campaign debate. It is interesting to note that the majority of listeners who heard the debate on radio credited Nixon with winning. However, those who watched the debates on television gave Kennedy the victory. Analysts attributed viewers' reaction of less confidence in what he said to Nixon's frequently shifting eye movements.

- Looking at one person for more than about five seconds makes the person feel as though he or she is being stared at and results in discomfort for that individual, especially if the message could be interpreted as harsh or scolding.

- Avoiding eye contact with your audience sends a message of guilt or the message that you're not leveling with the listeners.

- Be careful who you look at if what you're saying is "preachy" or could be considered a reprimand. A listener may conclude that your remarks are directed at her or him personally, and that you are using a public occasion to embarrass or get even with him.

- Establish eye contact with a person in one area of your audience, then move to another section, and so on. Concentrating on one part of the audience for an extended time makes people in other areas of the room feel left out.

- Conversely, looking at a person who has a "show me" look— arms folded, looking at a watch—can be disconcerting to you as a speaker. For your own mental health and speaking success, try to look at friendly faces with involved expressions.

- Being tied to your notes or script prohibits your making and maintaining good eye contact and results in less interest in your presentation. When reading from a book, hold the book up just below your chin, so that you can glance up every few seconds and look at your audience. Limit the length of the passage. Paraphrase part of it. The fine art of eye contact is a vital skill that must be developed in order to be a successful speaker. It can go a long way toward making you appear confident, personable, competent, honest, and in control.

Facial Expressions

Consider: The expression on your face reinforces what you are saying (or certainly should), adds subtle facets to your meaning, and can go a long way toward keeping the attention of your audience. An animated facial expression is a potent tool for involving your audience with you as a speaker.

Most people do not like to carry on really important conversations over the telephone. Do you know why? We want to see the other person's reaction to our words. And we want to be sure we understand his or her meaning. So we have to be looking at the other person as well as hearing his or her words. The voice alone doesn't tell the whole story.

Research has shown that a very high percentage of learning takes place through the sense of sight. Remember, the average person learns eighty-seven percent by sight. Hearing is the next highest means of learning, with only seven percent. Those figures should have a tremendous impact on what we do. As speakers, obviously we have to give our listeners something to see as well as to hear. And what they see and what they hear have to go together. Try looking in the mirror and saying, "Oh, I'm so happy" with a dour, sad expression; or say, "I'm terribly sad" with a lilt in your voice and a broad smile and see what kind of impression you make on yourself.

The expressionless speaker who stands in one position throughout a speech is inviting the audience's minds to wander to other things. If you don't give them something interesting to watch, they're going to be painting more interesting mental pictures in their mind's eye. Since the human face is supposedly capable of 250,000 different expressions, there should be no reason for a speaker to stand with a deadpan expression.

Reinforcing Your Words with Your Face

There are several benefits to using good facial expressions.

1. Facial expressions help you to set the mood for your audience. When you smile or laugh, you cue them to get ready for something light or less serious. With a somber expression, you help them prepare for something of a more serious nature.

2. Your expressions convey that you are human, that you have a personality, and that you are a regular person—just like your listeners.

3. Good facial expressions help your audience to follow your line of thought, and they alert the audience to what their reaction should be.

Here are some helpful hints on making facial expressions a real asset in speaking.

- Maintain an overall pleasant countenance—even if you're talking about a very serious subject. Speakers who frown and grimace the whole time make members of the audience feel as though they've been hit over the head with a bat.
- Make sure what you're saying with your face matches what you're saying with your tongue. If the two don't agree, the result can be confusing to your audience. But it also can be skillfully used to produce laughter, since incongruity is one service of humor.
- Use your facial expressions with reinforcing gestures to get and keep your audience's attention.
- Learn to be an actor—especially when telling anecdotes and using other illustrative material.
- Practice in front of a mirror or with video equipment.
- Make sure your facial expressions appear natural and spontaneous, not forced or contrived.
- Remember that you can convey friendliness and a genuine interest in your audience with the look on your face.
- In speaking, your face can truly be your fortune...if it's used to best advantage.

The way you dress, stand, move, gesture, look, and make eye contact all make very strong statements—at times louder than your words. It pays to make sure these visual impressions are not contradicting your message but are saying what you want the audience to understand.

Chapter 4

THE MECHANICS OF SPEAKING

So likewise you, unless you utter by the tongue words easy to understand, how will it be known what is spoken? For you will be speaking into the air (1 Cor. 14:9).

You are What You Eat

Consider: As a speaker, you are what you eat. Want to program yourself for failure as a speaker? Then eat a huge meal right before you speak. It's tough to be an after-dinner speaker and just sit and pick at your food—especially if it looks and smells delicious. But it's definitely the prudent thing to do.

When you eat a lot, your blood vessels shunt your blood supply to your digestive organs, away from other parts of your body. Since those include your brain, the result is a drop in mental sharpness and response. You experience post-prandial drowsiness, which is in direct proportion to how much you "pigged out." You also have, as a result, less physical energy—something every speaker needs in super-abundance.

As a speaker, you also need to be aware that the same things are happening to your audience if they've just eaten a big meal. You may have to use your ingenuity to keep them awake.

One speaker said, "In my travels abroad, I am frequently struck by the fact that most civilized nations allow for a sensible siesta after the noonday meal. The United States stands almost alone in its insistence upon a more rigorous approach. I refer, of course, to our quaint custom of forcing those who have just eaten heartily to digest a full-fledged speech along with their meat and potatoes."[1]

Some other cautions regarding food: Chocolate is particularly bad for the voice, and carbonated drinks can be hazardous to your speaking, especially if you have a tendency to burp. Nervousness will often result in a dry mouth and a tense throat, but the answer is not to drink ice water. That will only make the throat tighter. Taking a few sips of a warm drink is better. Or, if that's not available, bring your teeth down oh-so-carefully several times on your tongue (as though you're going to bite it). In a few seconds, there will be enough saliva to overcome a parched mouth.

Never...don't ever...whatever you do...don't drink any alcoholic beverages before you speak. If you do, there's one chance in a million that you'll come across as urbane and witty as you think you are.

Voice

Consider: Your voice is the instrument that you must use to convey your message. It has an infinite variety of pitches, levels, and tones. You need to learn to play on it just as an accomplished musician coaxes inspired and beautiful sounds from a violin.

Perhaps you have noticed how often we form opinions of others based on the sound of their voices. We say, "I have never met him, but he sounds nice over the phone."

Each person has been given a distinctive voice. That is one of the things that makes you unique. All of us can learn to use our voices more effectively, with training and concentrated effort. Few of us ever really develop the full potential of our vocal mechanisms to sway others in speaking.

A must for improving your speaking voice is a tape recorder. None of us sounds the way we think we do. If you're not accustomed to hearing your own voice as others hear it, the sound will be a real shocker at first. Listen and ask yourself this question: "Do I have the kind of voice, the enthusiasm, and the clarity in speaking that I would find easy to listen to?" If your answer is "no" or "not quite," now's the time to do something about it.

Remember what Fred Glanz, world champion hog caller, said: "You've got to have appeal as well as power in your voice. You've got to convince the hogs you've got something for them."

Vocal Energy

One of the most important things a speaker can do to keep attention is to maintain a high level of vocal energy throughout the presentation. Dynamically projecting your voice with power and zest, rather than merely letting the words fall out of your mouth, indicates enthusiasm and excitement. If you don't appear enthusiastic, why would anyone want to listen?

Mac Douglass said, "Burning desire will reflect itself in fiery words. Excitement and enthusiasm are essential to successful speaking and go hand in hand with a presenter's level of confidence."[2] It also has to do with the speaker's vocal energy. Regardless of how enthusiastic you may feel about your subject, unless you project that enthusiasm through a high level of vocal energy, your audience will never know.

Vocal Pitch

Do you sound as good as you look? After listening to yourself on the tape recorder, decide if your voice has any of these poor characteristics.

Breathy	Adolescent
Whiny	Nasal
Whispery	Screechy
High-pitched	Strident
Chirpy	Shrill

Or do you have a firm, strong, low-pitched, colorful voice? A low-pitched voice is soft, soothing, and persuasive. It also radiates power and commands attention.

Would you believe that long-time movie star Lauren Bacall once had a high-pitched voice? Not only high, but also high and nasal, according to the late Howard Hawks, the film director credited with giving Bacall her start in films.

When Hawks first met Bacall, the first thing he noticed as she asked for work was a tiny, nasal voice. "I had to be honest," he recalled. "I said that the lines we had, the stories, were not made for a high nasal voice." She left and, to his amazement, returned in about three weeks. When she said "Hello," she sounded like a different person. "I had to admire her," he recalled. "She wanted to work and she had to have put forth much time and effort to accomplish this."[3]

What if you, like Lauren Bacall, have a naturally high-pitched, irritating voice? You can do something about it.

The point is not to try to force your voice lower but to coax it down by relaxing your throat muscles. Tense throat muscles can create an artificially high voice. First of all, train your own ears to locate the proper pitch for your voice. Put your hand on your chest and lower your voice a half tone at a time on the phrase "I think it is not going to snow" until your throat gets uncomfortable. At that point, sensibly go back up one tone.

A good way to keep reminding yourself to stay at this lower level is match your vocal level with the corresponding note on a piano and then, from time to time, read aloud, striking the note again and again and matching your pitch to it.

To gently stretch and deepen your voice, say "King Kong, ding dong, bing bong." Each time go lower in tone so that your last "bong" is easing down into that strange gravelly range. Never force this sound! Just let it ease out. Bit by bit, your voice will be led down in tone, and some of the high-pitched tightness will leave your voice.

One cause of a higher-pitched voice is nervousness, which results in tensing the vocal cords and throat muscles. Fortunately there are exercises to relax your throat. Do them a couple of times a day until you can prove to your own satisfaction that you have lowered your pitch.

1. Sitting, let your head hang forward as though you had no neck supporting it. Shut your eyes for five very slow counts.

2. Lie on your back on the floor, knees bent. Concentrate on each part of your body—from feet to head—in sequence, willing it to relax. Breathe in to the slow count of six, and then gradually exhale to the slow count of six before going to the next part of your body.

3. Now sit up and, with your head rolling slowly in a circle, first clockwise and then counter-clockwise, say "I am relaxed. I am completely relaxed." Say it over and over again, starting with scarcely more than a whisper. Then, very gradually, increase your volume until you're speaking at a normal volume. You'll notice a lower pitch to your voice.

But what if your voice is nasal? The main cause of nasality is a tight jaw or tension in the muscles in the back of the tongue. If you don't open your mouth when you speak, the sound has to come through your nose.

These exercises will help overcome an unpleasant nasal twang.

1. Yawn elaborately, extravagantly, exaggeratedly. But remember to breathe normally and keep your shoulders and neck uninvolved.

2. Open your mouth only slightly, keeping your lower jaw as relaxed as possible. Then make an "ah" sound while moving your lower jaw rapidly from side to side.

3. To get accustomed to hearing your sound come out of your mouth instead of your nose, hold one palm in front of your lips and blow into it while saying "Whisssh." Say it over and over again. Your breath should be coming out in tiny explosions.

Vocal Range

Most people do not begin to take advantage of the full range of their speaking voices.

Speaking in a monotone voice—on basically the same pitch— can be an opiate to the listener and deadly dull, even if the nodders manage to keep their eyes open. Your listeners may wish to hear you next time they have insomnia, but chances are they won't want to hear you again as a speaker. A monotone speaker has little chance of getting his message across. He or she is just too hard to listen to.

Even if you aren't a Johnny-one-note speaker, you can improve your vocal range by concentrated effort.

Try selecting a passage to read. Find your most comfortable pitch on the piano, and then read the passage at a lower note and then a higher note. Go about three notes higher and three or four notes lower than your starting pitch. Then read the passage using the full range.

You might even want to try singing the passage (even if it's only in the shower) to really see how variety of pitch can enhance the color and meaning of your words.

Another interesting exercise is to choose a children's story with a variety of characters. Find an appropriate pitch level for each one; for example, a deep, guttural tone for the villain, and a high, tiny voice for a very young child or animal. Read the story using the appropriate voices for each character, preferably to an audience of a child or children.

Exploring your vocal range and experimenting with your voice will add variety to your speaking and gain greater interest on the part of your audience.

Vocal Level

People who fail to speak loudly enough communicate doubt and indecision to the listener. Listeners also get the impression that they are tired, lack energy, are unenthusiastic, or are in poor health.

Here are a couple of clues that you aren't speaking loudly enough.

Do others often ask you to repeat yourself?

Do they appear to be straining to hear you, possibly by leaning their heads a bit closer or turning an ear toward you?

Speaking up is vital to the public speaker. According to Edward J. Hegarty, a nationally known lecturer, "The voice that is difficult to hear doesn't show confidence, indicate enthusiasm or demonstrate leadership qualities."[4]

Here are some suggestions to ensure your listeners will actually hear what you say.

- Hold your head up. It's not likely that the listener will hear you if you're talking to your chest. Seeing the formation of your words also helps the other person understand what you are saying—especially if he or she has any kind of hearing problem.

- Project your voice. Throw it out to your audience, just as you would a baseball. Speak from your diaphragm. In normal conversation we use just chest tones, so we have to make a concerted effort to speak from the diaphragm. A good way to get used to using this technique is to practice this simple exercise. Place your hand on your diaphragm (located between your rib cages), take a deep breath so that you feel your diaphragm inflate like a balloon, then say "Ho, ho, ho" loudly. You should feel your diaphragm move with each "ho." Then say "Ha, ha, ha." Repeat several times.

- Open your mouth more widely. Closed-mouth talkers are difficult to understand. Practice talking with a wide-open mouth. Doing so will add volume to your voice.

- Assume that the listener is hard of hearing and that you'll have to speak a little louder to be heard. It is better to be slightly too loud than to be not loud enough.
- Be aware of noises you may have to overcome, such as air conditioning or a speaker in the meeting room next door.

Here are a few cautions about vocal level and the use of a microphone.

- Don't substitute a mike for good speaking techniques. You still need to project your voice.
- Be sure to speak into the mike and have it properly positioned, considering the type of microphone you're using.
- If you are a speaker who tends to become very loud at times, back slightly away from the mike at those times. You don't want to deafen the audience.
- Be sure the microphone level is appropriately set for you as a speaker. You should check it out before the meeting begins. It is also a good idea to have someone monitor the level while you are speaking since a room full of people alters the way sound carries. Although you want the level high enough, you should be sure it is not set so loud that you are actually hurting your listeners' ears.
- Don't forget to vary your volume level, making sure it's still being heard. Lowering your voice can produce a very intimate, confidential moment between the speaker and the audience. Getting louder can produce a dramatic build toward a climax. You might want to consider using a stage whisper for an especially dramatic statement.
- When using a microphone, be sure to enunciate even more clearly than usual.
- If a cordless mike is available, so much the better. Once you have it securely in place, you have the freedom to move around. Just be sure extra batteries are available in case the sound fizzles, leaving you mikeless.

Delivery Rate

Just as you need variety in pitch and speaking level, you also need to vary your speed in speaking.

As a whole, when speaking before an audience, you will want to speak a little bit faster than your normal conversational rate. There are several reasons for increasing your rate.

1. Your listener will be thinking at a rate four times faster than most people speak. A little more rapid pace will help compensate for this difference.

2. A more rapid pace projects enthusiasm and energy.

3. People are convinced that people who speak faster are brighter.

4. Experiments conducted by James MacLachlan showed that speaking somewhat faster than usual enhanced the speaker's persuasiveness, increased the speaker's ratings on trust and knowledge, and improved information recall among listeners. Overall, a twenty-five-percent increase in the speaker's delivery rate was preferred by a substantial majority of those tested.[5]

Here are some other important things to keep in mind about the pace you use in speaking.

*   If you are speaking away from your area of the country, keep in mind the speaking rate of your listeners. You should speak a little faster than they do—but not too much faster. Southerners, for example, accustomed to a slower rate of speech in everyday life, will have trouble adjusting to an extremely rapid-fire speaker. The opposite is also true. An eastern audience will go to sleep listening to a speaker from the South—especially one with a marked southern accent—unless the speaker makes a marked effort to speed up.

*   Speaking at the same rate all the time gets monotonous. Speed up. Slow down, especially when you want to emphasize a certain point.

*   And stop. Don't be afraid of silence. A dramatic pause can be more powerful at times than any words you might say. If you ask the audience a question, be quiet so that they really have time to reflect on your query and mentally answer your question.

*   Remember that without excellent diction, you cannot speak very rapidly and be easily understood.

Breath Control

Consider: Using your voice without adequate breath support is like an elephant's attempt to walk on sea-gull legs.

Has your voice ever gone completely out of control when you were nervous? Most people have had that experience at one time or another. What happens is that stage fright results in a souped-up respiratory rate. And the more shallowly we breathe, the less support we have for our voices.

Three types of breathing

Clavicular breathing comes from the top portions of the chest. It is the least desirable method for speakers because they cannot get sufficient air to last them through a complete thought. Clavicular breathing also does not provide the necessary support system to produce a well-modulated, controlled sound. This type of breathing usually tips the audience off that the speaker is nervous.

Thoracic breathing is normal chest breathing. Air quantity is sufficient for conversation and usual physical activity.

Abdominal or diaphragmatic breathing is the preferred type of breathing for public speaking because it maximizes the air quantity. In abdominal breathing, the abdominal muscles help expand the chest fully. Athletes use diaphragmatic breathing. They have to in order to run the race successfully.

Have you ever watched a baby breathe? Babies breathe from the diaphragm naturally. As we get older, most of us switch to thoracic breathing unless we have a need to breathe more deeply.

To practice breathing from the diaphragm, place your hand between the two halves of your rib cage and inhale. If you are breathing deeply enough, you should feel your diaphragm expand like a balloon. Exhale and you will feel it go down. Another good way to check your breathing is to lie down on your back and place a lightweight book on your stomach. It should go up and down as you breathe.

If you are not accustomed to abdominal breathing, build up to it gradually. Too much deep breathing to begin with can result in dizziness.

There are several major benefits to be gained from breathing from the diaphragm.

1. First, breathing from the diaphragm has a calming effect on your entire mind, body, and emotions. The opposite is true of shallow breathing.

2. Breathing from the diaphragm gives you control over your voice. It helps your voice to mind you.

3. It provides the support your voice needs. This support is especially important for those who speak, sing, or otherwise use their voices extensively.

4. It results in a richer, fuller, more resonant tone. The contraction of the diaphragm enlarges the chest cavity. The larger chamber enables you to produce a fuller, rounder speaking voice that projects better.

5. Speaking from the diaphragm allows you to speak with greater intensity and provides greater range for dramatic emphasis. Try it for yourself. Say "What do you mean?" as you normally would. Then say the same sentence from the diaphragm.

There are several things you can do to develop the habit of breathing from the diaphragm and to control the flow of your breath in speaking. Here are some suggestions.

• Inhale on the count of five. Hold your breath for a count of five. Then exhale, saying "ea-sy" slowly.

• Inhale. Exhale evenly on a count of ten.

• Tighten the diaphragm muscles about your waist as if someone were about to punch you and you wanted to block the blow. Release. Breathe fairly deeply so your ribs expand to the sides and back. Then tighten those diaphragm muscles and exhale slowly with control to a count of ten, twenty, thirty, forty—whatever length you can comfortably handle. Make a hissing sound, "ssss," through your teeth as you do it. This exercise is also a good relaxation exercise.

Diction

Consider: We read in the Bible the following question: "So likewise you, unless you utter by the tongue words easy to understand, how will it be known what is spoken? For you will be speaking into the air" (I Cor. 14:9).

What you say is important, but the way you say your words is critical—if you are to be understood. Unfortunately, most Americans are lip-lazy in comparison with many people from other countries. Have you ever really watched a Frenchman speak? He makes all kinds of faces and uses his lips energetically, non-stop. He has to, in order to form the sounds in his language correctly.

We need to take a cue from the Frenchman in order to produce the sounds of the English language correctly...and so that they can be easily understood. Mumblers chew their words and don't use the facial muscles necessary for clear enunciation.

Here are some suggestions for improving the clarity of your speech.

1. Practice reading aloud with a tape recorder and actually hear where you need to improve. Increase your speed, reading as rapidly as you possibly can while still forming your sounds correctly and understandably.

2. Open your mouth when you speak.

3. Move your lips.

4. Practice putting on the final consonant sounds. Omitting final consonants is probably the most common mistake in enunciation. Often a speaker will end up saying something entirely different from what he means. For example, if the speaker says, "Sometimes a little help is all a person needs," but fails to put the "p" on the word "help," the listener will definitely get a different message from the one intended.

5. Also, watch beginning consonants. Some speakers have a habit of occasionally dropping initial consonants, and this habit can also be dangerous.

6. Be sure you are forming vowel sounds properly. These are some good words to practice in this regard.

   • Mate, mote, mute, moot
   • Rack, reck, rock, ruck, rook
   • Bah, boil, beau, boo

7. There are a number of often used, simple words that are commonly mispronounced. Practice saying these words correctly:

   • arctic   • creek
   • February   • government

- roof
- congratulate
- fifth
- strength
- perhaps

- what
- dais
- manufacture
- education
- library

Pay particular attention to words ending in "ing." All too often "going to" comes out "gonna," and "running" sounds like "runnen." Also, take care in saying the word "you." Far too many speakers say "don't cha" instead of "don't you."

8. Then there are the charlatan words, that masquerade as words but really aren't words at all. Some of the most common are these:

- irregardless for regardless
- wisht for wish
- accidently for accidentally
- anywheres for anywhere
- furtherest for furthest
- hunderd for hundred
- unawares for unaware
- heighth for height
- undoubtably for undoubtedly

9. A good exercise for improving enunciation and projection is the whisper drill. While whispering, exaggerate the functions of the mouth, lips, and tongue. To be heard across the room, the speaker will be forced to make a clean break between all the words. He or she will need to slow this whispered speech to the point that the vocal muscles can manage each word distinctly.

10. Listen to good speakers—on the platform, on television, on the radio. Notice how meticulously they speak...correctly yet not pedantically. Also, learn from the mistakes you notice in other speakers. As you begin to clean up and polish your diction, your speech will seem stilted, perhaps ostentatious. But before long, you will find yourself speaking correctly as a matter of course.

11. Be on the lookout for slovenly speech. Snap off the ends of your words. Put crispness into your words. Show purpose in each word you utter. Most of all, don't let your method of

speaking sabotage the message of your speech. Remember Shakespeare's admonition: "Speak the speech I pray you... trippingly on the tongue."

Silence—the Pause that Refreshes

Consider: Oliver Wendell Holmes said, "Talking is like playing the harp. There is as much in laying the hands on the strings to stop their vibration as in twanging them to bring out their music."[6]

Unfortunately, too many would-be orators think it is absolutely necessary to hear the sound of their voices at all times—without pause or relief to the audience. As a result, they keep talking—even when they don't have words to say. This practice results in a steady stream of non-words or meaningless fillers, which in over-abundance can be very distracting—even extremely annoying to the listener.

The sad thing is that using filler sounds can become such a deeply ingrained habit that the speaker is not even aware it's a problem. But the audience will be very much aware that it is a problem. In fact, when the habit is carried to extremes, the audience may even tune out the message because of the mess of meaningless sounds.

Probably the worst culprit is "uh" or "er." Frances Rodman tells us that "many after-dinner speakers remind us that to 'er-r' is human."[7] Dorothy Sarnoff whimsically quotes Genesis 38:7: "Er was wicked in the sight of the Lord; and the Lord slew him." She maintains that "the Lord was right. To err is human, but to 'er' should be considered a capital crime. My only complaint about the slaying of Er is that it should have been done before he had a chance to start a family; his descendants today threaten to take over the world."[8]

There's no doubt about it. "Er" does have a whole family with criminal tendencies. How many times have you suffered through a tirade of words like these: "uh," "like," "y'know," "see what I mean," "o.k.?" "well," "man," "right?"

Not as bad, but not good either, is an endless stream of unnecessary connector words like "and," "so," "well," "now," and "OK." These words can turn several paragraphs into one long, out-of-control sentence. Perhaps you've had the experience of listening to speakers who never end a sentence. It can become a game almost, wondering when they're going to have to pause long enough to come up for air.

A word or phrase used repetitively can become filler material also and be almost as distracting. Think about your pet phrases and start noticing whether you use them excessively in conversation. If so, you no doubt will do the same thing before an audience.

The remedy for these common maladies—short of gagging the speaker—is silence, the pause that refreshes. There are several benefits of using a pause in speaking.

1. Whereas filler sounds distract your audience, pausing periodically will call your audience's attention more forcefully to the words you say.

2. Silence is the punctuation of speech, just as a semicolon, a period, or a new paragraph is of written communication. Silence lets the audience know when you've come to the end of a thought, when you're ready to make a transition.

3. A carefully placed pause will allow you to drive your points home. A pause gives the audience time to absorb your points and reflect on what you've said.

4. The pause gives you, as a speaker, an opportunity to collect your thoughts and to move around if you start feeling tense.

5. A moment of silence also gives you time to catch your breath and enables you to use your voice more effectively.

Sandy Livner, president of a public speaking firm, believes that pauses are very important tools in speaking effectively. She says, "A person who knows how to pause at the right time—who controls a period of silence—comes across as being more authoritative than the person who doesn't."[9]

George Jessel said that he learned his best trick from George M. Cohan who "taught me how to pause while talking to an audience so as to make them believe that I was thinking of something important, or some new line that had just come to mind—when it was actually something tried and true that I knew should get a laugh."[10]

The following tips are some good things to remember about eliminating filler sounds and meaningless words, and about using the pause effectively.

- Chances are, if you use padding as a public speaker, you also use it in conversation. Since awareness is the first step toward correcting the habit, get your spouse or a close friend to help you become conscious of the extent of your habit. Get someone you're around a lot to give you a silent signal—for example, pulling the ear or touching the nose—each time you use a speech filler.

- Check yourself out with a tape recorder. Tell a story and play it back. You may be surprised by how many times you say "uh" and "you know." Even better, next time you speak in public have someone record your remarks and listen to them when you get home.

- Silence can be used to give your presentation more impact and to add interest. A dramatic pause can be a potent tool for a speaker. Use the pause to give emphasis to a certain word or phrase in a sentence. Silence can help build suspense, especially in telling a story.

- Silence can be used as an effective attention-getting device. If several people are looking around, stop talking. You'll get their attention. Silence also can be used to stop a distracting activity of audience members. For example, if two people are talking, stop and look at them. Chances are it won't be long before they'll grow uncomfortable and become silent themselves.

- Be sure to pause briefly after each sentence, and longer after each paragraph. There are some cautions, however, in using the pause. Don't pause so much that it seems as it there are gaps in your speech pattern. And don't pause so long that it seems as it as it you've forgotten your speech.

Differences in Oral and Written Language

Consider: Even though you may be an excellent writer, you will not be an excellent speaker if you use the same approach for speaking and writing. Oral and written languages are quite different in several ways.

- Written language must be ultimately intelligible to the reader. Spoken language must be instantly intelligible to the listener. A reader can go back and reread a sentence several times. As a speaker, though, you only have one chance to be understood.

- Spoken language is less formal. The style used in public speaking should lie somewhere between the written word and conversation.
- Spoken language is more repetitive. It is important to rephrase several times key ideas you want the listeners to take away with them.
- Spoken language is more idiomatic. Otherwise, it sounds somewhat stilted and stuffy.
- Spoken language should be simpler in structure than written language is. The subject, verb, and object must stand out in spoken sentences and not be overwhelmed by a lot of parenthetical clauses. Otherwise, the listener will have a hard time following your train of thought.
- Spoken language is more likely to include questions.
- The length of sentences in spoken language is less uniform. Short sentences are shorter. Long sentences are longer.
- Oral language uses more contractions.
- Figurative language adds life and color to spoken words. Imaginative metaphors, similes, and alliteration can turn an otherwise pedestrian speech into a memorable one. Consider these examples of figurative language:

    - Lincoln described a nation "conceived in liberty."
    - Kennedy spoke of freedom as a "torch passed to a new generation."[11]
    - J. F. Bere, chairman of Borg-Wagner Corporation, described untapped human assets as "waiting like a coiled spring to release enormous potentials." Problems were discussed as "smoldering fires" and new programs as being structured "a brick here, a brick there."[12]

- There's also a difference in rhythm. Take a cue from the musician who uses rhythm and cadence to intrigue listeners and to move the music to a climax. The speaker can also involve listeners and stir them, by the sheer force of the rhythm and cadence of the language, to heights of grandeur. The repetition of a word, a phrase, or a statement has an effect like that of a repeated theme in music with variations.

Rhythm

A good example comes from a speech given by U.S. Circuit Judge Abner J. Mikva: "These are trying times for all of us, yet I believe that trying times are a time to try. Not a time to shrug a shoulder in disgust and turn your back on the problems. Not a time to say that things are in a mess and will probably just get worse. And most definitely not a time to conclude that there is nothing a single individual can do."[13]

One of the classics of effective rhythm is Martin Luther King's speech, "I Have a Dream". He used the phrase "I have a dream" seven times, preceding phrases such as "every valley shall be exalted," "every hill and mountain shall be made low," "the rough places will be made plain," and "the glory of the Lord shall be revealed." He also used the phrase "Let freedom ring" ten times.[14]

Can you find a more beautiful passage in literature than the Beatitudes? Jesus began each statement with the words, "Blessed are...." Then the statements moved from the present tense to the future tense. In that same chapter He repeatedly alluded to his authority over Pharisaic traditions with His words, "You have heard. But I say to you."

Since a written speech must be read, it is important to read it aloud to check for the flow of words and phrases and for spots that may be difficult to get your tongue around.

A well crafted, dynamic presentation can be a special gift to your audience. Make sure that you, as the delivery system, present it to the receiver in the best condition and the most effective manner possible.

Chapter 5

CONNECTING WITH YOUR AUDIENCE

For though I am free from all men, I have made myself a servant to all, that I might win the more. And to the Jews I became as a Jew, that I might win Jews; to those who are under the law, as under the law, that I might win those who are under the law; to those who are without law, as without law (not being without law toward God, but under law toward Christ), that I might win those who are without law; to the weak I became as weak, that I might win the weak. I have become all things to all men, that I might by all means save some. Now this I do for the gospel's sake, that I may be partaker of it with you. (1 Cor. 9:19-23).

Finding Your Common Ground with Your Audience

Consider: You can be the most polished speaker in the world and still fall flat on your face if you leave out one of the most important ingredients of a successful speech—finding out everything possible about your audience and tailoring your content, techniques, and involvement approaches to their needs and intellectual level.

Someone has wisely said, "An effective speech starts where the audience is and ends where the speaker wants them to be." Failing to find out, in advance, where the audience is guarantees a less-than-effective speech.

If you've ever tried to use exactly the same speech with two very different types of audiences, you have probably learned the wisdom of adapting your remarks to the level and interests of each group. Of course, that's a part of the challenge and excitement of public speaking: learning how to move a particular audience to your point of view.

The world of advertising understands this principle well. Professionals in this field carefully target potential customers. The Volvo advertising campaign, for example, emphasizes different benefits for different audiences: economy and durability in America, leisure and status in France, performance in Germany, and safety in Switzerland.[1]

Volvo's advertisers know they can sell more cars if they appeal to the distinctive mindset and interests of the people they're trying to reach.

Making the Connection

It's important to find your common ground with your audience. Every speech begins with the speaker...

here...   and the audience...   over there.

In order to communicate effectively, you have to move closer together. The secret is to find some things you have in common with your audience, to move to "common ground."

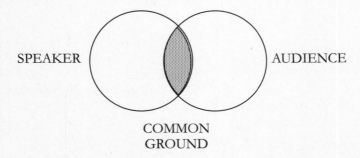

Each speech, in order to be effective, must be tailor-made for that particular audience.

Your first step in ensuring a successful experience—both for you and your audience—is to find out who will be listening to you, where they're coming from, and as much as possible about that particular occasion.

Consider the Logistics.

1. You need to know, first of all, about how many people will be there. Knowing the size of the audience is important for several reasons. First, the style of presentation will vary with the audience's size. In general, the larger the audience is, the more formal the presentation. Also, the size of the audience determines the effectiveness of various audiovisual approaches. For example, because of visibility limitations, it is impossible to use a dry-erase board or flip chart with a large group of people. Video and PowerPoint presentations may not be possible in a large facility unless a large-screen projection unit is available. Of course, if several closed-circuit video displays are being used for a huge audience, such as one at a large conference or convention, the style would become less formal, and close-ups of audiovisual aids could even enlarge the image.

    Successful audience participation techniques vary with the number of people. As a rule of thumb, the larger the audience is, the more difficult it is to get participation. Audience size will also determine whether or not you may want to use handout materials and what type of materials would be appropriate.

2. Knowing about the facility is vital to the success of your presentation. These are some things you will want to know in advance.

    -   How will listeners be seated? In formal, stationary rows or in small groups? Will there be tables providing a surface on which they may write? How much leeway, if any, will you have to restructure the seating configuration?

    -   Will you be on a raised platform or on floor level with the participants?

    -   Will there be a stationary mike or, preferably, a cordless mike allowing you to move around? Purchasing your own cordless mike is an excellent investment.

- How are the acoustics? If the group is relatively small, the acoustics are good, and you project well, you may want to consider speaking without a microphone.

- Is this a meeting at which a meal will be served?

- Will you be seated on the platform or with the group before you speak?

- Is audiovisual equipment available if you wish to use it? Can it be used effectively in this particular setting?

- Is the setting outdoors? Take into account complications that may arise: distracting background noises, a very informal atmosphere, perhaps a sudden cloudburst. Also, realize that, because sound is dispersed, laughter is more difficult to generate.

- Will there be other speakers on the program? If so, where will your presentation be in the order of the program?

- How much time has been set aside in the program for your presentation? Be sure to abide by the time limit given. Time your remarks as you prepare. Be aware that they probably will be slightly longer when you actually deliver them because of pauses for effect or audience reaction, such as applause, or laughter. If you're going to err, make it a little on the short side.

Even if you have not been given a time limit, consider the ability of your audience to sit still and concentrate. There is real truth in the saying "The mind can comprehend only what the seat can endure." Mark Twain pointed out the pitfalls of being long-winded:

> When the speaker had talked ten minutes I was so impressed I decided I would give every cent I had with me. After another ten minutes I concluded that I would throw into the treasury all the silver I had about me. Ten minutes later I decided I wouldn't give anything, and at the end of the talk, still ten minutes later, as the contribution plate came around, I was so utterly exhausted by the arguments that I extracted two dollars for my own use.[2]

If you're tempted to go on and on, consider the fate of U.S. President William Henry Harrison. His inaugural address in 1841 was 9,000 words long. In the freezing cold, he spent two full hours in its delivery. He came down with pneumonia and died a month later. Laurie Rozakis said that the moral of the story is that "a speaker who is going to go on for hours better have a good speech, deliver it well, and stay out of the cold."[3]

Doing an Audience Analysis

There are four main areas where you can find common ground with your listeners:

- Common needs
- Shared interests
- Mutual concerns
- Same experiences

In order to find that common ground, it's essential that you have a good idea of who will be there and that you know as much as possible about them.

1. Ethnicity of the Group

Will several ethnic or racial groups be represented, or only one? When you are speaking to a group from a background other than your own, it's important to find ways to bridge the gap between your cultures. Try using anecdotes featuring persons of their ethnicity in a positive and successful light. Quote a well-known leader from their background. A historical reference giving credit for accomplishment can be effective. Or, if possible, relate a meaningful story from your own experience.

If the language of the audience's native country is not English, learn a few words in that language so that you may at least greet them in their tongue. Even if they are not fluent in that language themselves, they will appreciate your thoughtfulness. And you will have gone a long way toward building rapport and getting off on the right foot with them.

If the group's ethnicity is one with which you are unfamiliar, conduct some research. Interview the person who invited you to speak, and learn about their mores, mindsets, and usual manner of response. Ask someone to check the material you plan to use for the appropriateness of any areas that could be potentially sensitive or offensive to the group.

Speaking in another language can be even more challenging. Take the two biblical phrases "Your sins shall be white as snow" and "I am the bread of life," for example. John Beekman has convincingly defended the practice of translating these, for certain cultural groups, as "Your sins shall be white as cotton" and "I am the tortilla of life." Beekman explains:

> Many groups in Mexico consider bread to be second best and inferior to tortillas, or look upon it as dessert or party food. This function does not correspond to the idea Jesus had in mind.... To use a literal equivalent for bread in spite of its incompatible functional meaning, introduces a wrong equivalence.[4]

Also in Latin America, biblical terminology has been reworked for various Indian cultures. Thus parables about foxes (Matthew 8:20) have become parables about coyotes in Mazahua, Mexico; locusts (Mark 1:6) are changed to flying ants in Ayutla Mixteco, Mexico; and pulque replaces wine (Matthew 9:17) in Mezquital Otomi, Mexico. Also, people stick out their chins in place of shaking their heads (Mark 15:29) in Huitoto, Peru; and calling from the door replaces knocking (Acts 12:17) in Chol, Mexico.[5]

When speaking in another country, you have a better chance of being understood correctly if you do not use colloquial expressions. Avoid figurative speech like the plague.

2. Gender Makeup

Will your audience be all male, all female, or, in all likelihood, a mixture? If your listeners are in church, there will probably be more women than men. As a rule of thumb, men are more receptive to facts; women, to people-related information.

Alice Mathews recommends three approaches for connecting with women, particularly if you're a male speaker:

Translate masculine illustrations into feminine illustrations. Mathews writes about an amusing incident in speaking to a mixed audience in a Sunday church service. She used an illustration about her sewing machine. She stopped about halfway through her story and said, "I know that this baffles some of you men, but you need to know that this is my sweet revenge for all the sports illustrations

I've had to listen to all of my life." She reported that first there was a titter, then a roar of laughter followed by applause.[6]

Does Mathews' anecdote suggest you should never use an illustration related to sports? No, but try following it with one that probably would be of more interest to most women. Jesus was very careful to do so, often telling a story about a man and then one featuring a woman.

Translate abstract principles into terms of concrete relationships. Mathews continues, "My life is about people, a lot of lonely, confused and hurting people. I want to know how biblical principles work in my world....Effective communicators to women translate abstract principles by using illustrations drawn from relationships."[7]

Translate masculine language to feminine language. Mathews recalls the profound impact she experienced when a woman speaker changed the noun and pronoun from masculine to feminine as she quoted 2 Corinthians 5:17: "Therefore if any woman is in Christ, she is a new creation; old things have passed away; behold, all things have become new."

> I sat there stunned, then realized that tears were running down my cheeks. This meant me. I was included. Had you asked me ten minutes earlier if I were included in the text of 2 Corinthians 5:17, I would have said, "Of course!" Intellectually, I can grasp that. Emotionally, I cannot. A preacher who cares about communicating to women will not draw back from reiterating the text with feminine pronouns here and there.[8]

Jesus did that, too. He referred to the woman who had been bowed over for many years as "a daughter of Abraham." Men had always been referred to as "sons of Abraham," but women had not been called Abraham's daughters. Jesus, by translating masculine language to feminine language, let women know that they, too, were included in God's covenant with Abraham.

3. Occupations and Educational Levels

What are your audience's average educational background and level of sophistication? These levels should be kept in mind in your choice of terms, vocabulary, and audiovisual approaches.

However, regardless of the audience's background, simple language, imaginatively used, can be elegant and understandable to all. Speaking before a large group is not a good occasion to try to show off your outstanding vocabulary or to demonstrate your skill in constructing masterfully complex sentences. Some may be impressed, but most will be turned off and will tune you out. Interesting speakers don't always use profound language," writes Muriel Larson.

> They know how to speak to the level of their audiences, neither mystifying them with big words nor insulting their intelligence.... Even if we do have big vocabularies, we are wise to use simple words when we speak. Even people with keen intellects find it easier to listen to plain talk. Short words and sentences don't strain our brains. When words and sentences sound complicated, we tend to drift quietly off into thoughts of our own.[9]

Roy Alexander pointed out that President John F. Kennedy was quite deliberate in his choice and use of words. "He wanted both his message and his language to be plain and unpretentious, but never patronizing. He avoided 'suggest,' 'perhaps,' and 'possible alternatives for consideration'....Kennedy used little or no slang, dialect, legalisms, contractions, clichés, elaborate metaphors, or ornate speech."

Alexander quotes Theodore Sorensen, Kennedy's speechwriter:

> Our criterion was always audience comprehension and comfort. This meant: (1) short speeches, short clauses, and short words, wherever possible; (2) a series of points or propositions in numbered or logical sequence, wherever appropriate; and (3) the construction of sentences, phrases, and paragraphs to simplify, clarify, and emphasize.[10]

The preaching of Dwight L. Moody provides a good example of using simple words. His sermons were analyzed for the complexity of language he used. The results showed that approximately seventy-nine percent of the words he employed were of one syllable, sixteen percent were two syllables, and only four percent were three syllables.[11]

Knowing the occupations of your listeners will also be helpful in selecting anecdotal material and approaches. This principle is especially true if you are speaking in an area with a concentration of people in one field or in similar fields. For example, with a primarily blue-collar group, an analogy describing plumbing or an earth-moving machine would probably have more meaning than one about the endeavors of a rocket scientist. Charts, tables, and graphs impress highly technical, well educated audiences. With a lower-level group, the more authoritarian the speaker, the better he or she will be accepted.

Should you take a mainly factual, logical approach or a more inspirational, idea and emotion-sparking tack? Professionals in engineering and accounting will, for the most part, respond more positively to the former, while those in social services or the arts will usually be more greatly moved by the latter approach.

4. Age Factor

It is important to know ahead of time the age distribution of the group you will face. Will it include children and teens as well as adults? Will the adults represent several different generations? Knowing the typical viewpoints, needs, interests, and mindsets of the various groups can go a long way in helping to plan an effective presentation.

George Barna cautions that scriptural references may not have the impact on young listeners that we intend:

> Relatively few of the Busters and late Boomers know the names of the books of the Bible or even the most basic or popular Scriptural passages. While the Word of God instructs, it pierces and it empowers us; if carelessly used in preaching to a biblically illiterate audience it may also unnecessarily discourage or repulse the listener—not because of the content of the Word, but because of how such references were used in the communication.[12]

The younger generation's views on illustrative material also need to be taken into consideration. Barna claims that young listeners are turned off by too many quotations or historical or literary references, because the younger generation is less familiar with classic works of literature, the names of literary or spiritual giants, and with the basics of world history than are older Americans.[13] Barna also says that information conveyed through the use of technology often has a higher degree of believability for younger people than does spoken information.[14]

What are the special interests, affiliations, and religious backgrounds of your audience? Is this a group of new converts? seekers? mature

Christians? or a mixture?

A good technique is to profile an average member of your audience by asking yourself these questions.

- Who is he?
- Why is she listening to me?
- What does he want or need?
- What does she like?
- What does he already know?
- What does she believe?
- What is his self-image?
- What is her image of me?
- What are his interests?
- What is her language, including slang and jargon?
- What motivates him?
- How much will she be interested in knowing about my subject?
- How can I get his attention?
- How can I keep her interested in what I have to say?

Other helpful questions include the following:

1. What is of special importance or concern in the life and work of this group at this particular time?

2. Have any notable accomplishments been made by the congregation or organization, or by members within the group recently?

3. Is this a special occasion? If so, get some background information from the person who asked you to speak.

4. What is the group's express purpose in inviting you to speak?

5. If the speaking engagement is out of town, what of significance is happening at that particular time in that community? Looking over current copies of the local newspaper in advance can help you get a feel for the community's "climate." Mentioning something the community is particularly proud of, such as its high school team's state championship victory, can be an instant rapport-builder.

6. What does the group know about you? What might be their attitude toward you and/or your group?

7. Why were you asked to speak on this particular topic (if you were given a special subject)? If you were not given a specific topic, what subject would be of particular interest to these listeners?

8. How much does the group already know about your subject? You do not want to insult their intelligence if they are already knowledgeable on the subject, but neither do you want to speak over their heads.

9. What are the attitudes of the group about your subject? Do they have any specific interests in relation to this topic?

10. Do they have strongly held beliefs and mindsets you would want either to address or to avoid?

11. Are there any especially sensitive feelings or any recent local events that might relate to the subject of your speech?

12. Would a question-and-answer session be appropriate? If so, will additional time for the session be provided or should you include it in your allotted time?

13. Are you speaking away from home? Avoid colloquialisms that may not be understood. Be aware that expressions common to your part of the country can have a different meaning in another area—especially an audience in another country. A case in point is the Londoner who was asked to say a few words at a luncheon in Taipei. Since he did not speak Chinese, his remarks were translated by an interpreter. His words "I just want you to know that I'm tickled to death to be here," came out in translation, "This poor man scratches himself until he dies, only to be with you."

A Helpful Analysis

If you will be speaking to a group with whom you are not familiar, this form should be helpful:

AUDIENCE ANALYSIS FORM

Name of Group _____

Date _____

Time _____

Place _____

Number of Persons Expected _____

Makeup of Group (Ethnicity, Gender, Educational Background, Interests, Occupations, etc.) _____

Group's Purpose in Calling You to Speak _____

_____

Topic of Speech _____

Group's Knowledge of the Subject _____

_____

Group's Attitude Toward Subject _____

_____

Other Presentations to Be Given _____

Question and Answer Session? _____

Features of Meeting Room _____

Arrangements for Audiovisuals _____

Group's Attitude Toward You _____

Sensitive Local Topics or Recent Events _____

_____

_____

Audience Analysis—an Ongoing Process

All of the previously discussed approaches to analyzing your audience should be done before the speaking engagement. However, audience analysis should not end there. It should continue as you arrive at the event; before your speech begins; while others are eating, speaking, or what have you; and even during your speech.

On Arrival

Plan to arrive early to check the "lay of the land." Arriving early is especially important if you are speaking in an unfamiliar setting or to a group you do not know. Talk to as many persons as you can before the meeting begins. In this way you will gain a feel for the group and will build rapport. It also is nice to see a few friendly faces staring back at you instead of a roomful of strangers. An excellent rapport-builder is to mention a member of the group by name and tell what he or she said to you about your subject before the meeting.

Observe what takes place in the meeting before you speak. Note what other speakers before you do. Listen and look to evaluate the group's reaction to various speaking approaches. For example, if they are not very responsive in reacting to humor, you might want to leave out any jokes that will be really disastrous if no one laughs.

During Your Presentation

While you are speaking, watch your listeners like a hawk. Are they giving you clues that they're uncomfortable by: fanning, putting on jackets, rubbing their arms? If so, have the room temperature adjusted.

Are you keeping their attention? If they're looking at their watches (or even worse, holding them up to their ears to see if they're still running), fidgeting, or nodding you need to do something, and quick.

Here are some signs of inattention and some possible remedies.

Signal: Nodding heads.
Solution: Lower room temperature; increase your volume; ask the group to raise their hands, stand, or say a word or phrase to a neighbor; move out into the audience.

Signal: Persons whispering.
Solution: Quit talking yourself and look directly at the talkers. Usually the silence will get their attention, and they will become uncomfortable and quit chattering. If that doesn't work, ask one of them a question.

Signal: Puzzled looks on faces.
Solution: Restate your point in simpler language; give an illustration; show how what you've said relates to something in the listeners' experience; use a diagram or a drawing if a dry-erase board, a flip chart, or an overhead transparency is readily available.

Signal: Questions being asked that have already been answered, or irrelevant remarks.
Solution: Take a different approach in restating your position; in case of a persistent questioner or an argumentative person, offer to discuss the question afterwards.

Signal: People looking at watches or at clock at back of room.
Solution: Summarize the remainder of your talk, take a break, or do something totally unexpected.

Be alert to body language. What are they saying back to you as you speak? These are some generally accepted messages listeners give a speaker by what they do.

- Folding arms across chest—closed mind or hostile response
- Moving chair forward, leaning forward toward speaker—open-mindedness, interest in message
- Crossing legs—competitive attitude, opposition
- Stroking chin—undecided, contemplating
- Stroking cheek—receptive
- Open hands—willingness to listen
- Hands behind head—taking it all in
- Fidgeting, looking around—bored
- Swinging foot in circle, tapping foot—bored, impatient
- Wrinkled brow—puzzled, contemplating
- Wringing hands—nervous, anxious
- Twiddling thumbs—bored
- Shrugging shoulders—indifference
- Gritting teeth—anger
- Rolling eyes—disgust
- Dropping mouth open—disbelief
- Covering mouth with hand—surprise, shock

- Biting lip—concentration, thinking
- Looking off in distance—indifference, daydreaming
- Touching nose with index finger quickly—doubt
- Glancing sideways, drawing back—suspicion
- Placing fingertips together, like a steeple—confidence
- Become an eye watcher. The size of a person's pupils can give you a definite clue to how he or she is reacting to your ideas. Research shows that pupils dilate when persons react positively to what they hear or see and constrict when their response is negative.

A DIRTY DOZEN
(THINGS THAT TURN LISTENERS OFF)

1. A know-it-all attitude
2. Talking down to an audience… or talking way over their heads
3. Using too-big words, acronyms, and terminology they aren't familiar with
4. Over-persuasion, overselling—the speaker who clobbers the audience
5. A woman who tries to act like "one of the boys"
6. A speaker who smokes or drinks coffee or a cold drink while speaking (although taking an occasional sip of water to wet your throat is perfectly acceptable)
7. Repetitious movements, such as rocking or pacing
8. A speaker who blocks the view of visual material
9. Profane language and material
10. A speaker who plays with pencil, hair, mike cord, tie, etc.
11. Put-downs of audience or any group of people
12. A speaker who cannot easily be heard

Audience Involvement

Consider: People are much more likely to be supportive of something they're made to feel a part of. Involving your audience is one of the smartest things you can do to make your presentation a success.

Involving the listener in your presentation gives the impression that you care very much about communicating with him or her as an individual—that you're not just up there to talk to faceless forms and to hear your own voice. Involving the listener also shows your professionalism in spending the time necessary to plan strategies to reach and involve that particular group.

As a result of your efforts, your audience will feel included as an integral part of the presentation; and they will feel that your presentation was exactly tailored to fit their particular group.

There are many strategies you can use to get your audience significantly involved in what you're saying.

1.   Have them give another round of applause for someone who has just finished performing—another speaker, the master of ceremonies, a singer. This not only involves the audience; it makes you look good when you give credit to someone else on the program.

2.   Look for their "trophy case," something you can compliment them on. This could be a successful completion of a church building-fund campaign, a community project of a service club, improved attendance, or whatever. Have those involved stand and give them a hand. Or, if the whole group participated in the accomplishment, have them applaud themselves.

3.   Tell your listeners what's in it for them as individuals, how what you will say can improve their life. Research has shown that people are most concerned about health, safety, and money. Try to appeal to their concerns and aspirations.

4.   Hit your audience's "hot button." Use an illustration about something that really turns them on, that they have a burning interest in.

5.   Use examples, quotes, or anecdotes about people you know the audience holds in high esteem and identifies with. In the case of a particular ethnic group, quote a leader—for example, a congressperson of that race. If you're speaking to a women's group, use an outstanding, successful woman as an example. Or talk about a person from their city or state.

6. Use the names of people in the audience. For example, you might say, "I'm sure that as a trial lawyer, Sara can tell you the importance of learning to think on your feet." Mention something someone in the audience said that relates to your topic. Tell a story, even if it's hypothetical, about audience members. But either get their permission first or be very sure they will not be embarrassed and will enjoy the reference.

7. Show concern for your audience's comfort and convenience. If the room seems to be getting too warm, ask how many are uncomfortable and request that the thermostat be adjusted.

8. Get and maintain good eye contact with listeners in various sections of the audience.

9. Use the pronoun "you" a lot. Talk about "we." Reveal something about yourself. "Confess" that you have that same problem. All these approaches bridge the distance between the podium and the seats and build bonds of friendship.

10. Humor is an excellent means of gaining involvement. Sharing a good laugh makes everyone feel warm and friendly.

11. Have audience members raise their hands. Ask questions like these: "How many of you are native Dallasites?...or Methodists?" Or ask a piercing question such as this: "How many of you have ever felt like leaving your spouse?" And then very quickly say, "No, don't answer that question."

12. Have some members of the audience stand, or have the whole audience stand—particularly if they seem inattentive or appear to be getting drowsy in a hot, crowded room.

13. Have the audience repeat together a key word or key phrase you're discussing. However, doing this over and over can get boring.

14. Have listeners turn to their neighbors and tell them an important statement you want to highlight.

15. Give emphasis by saying that what you are going to tell them next is very important.

16. Give your listeners a mental task to perform. For example, ask them to think of their biggest problem and how what you just said relates to it. If there is time, see if someone would like to share their thought with the audience.

17. At a certain point, dramatically remove an article of clothing such as shoes, a coat, or a tie. For example, a school superintendent got the audience in the palm of his hand when he talked to administrators about the importance of seeing everything through the eyes of the classroom teacher. He took off his coat when he told of going back to the classroom and teaching a class every day himself so he could get back in touch with the challenges and problems teachers face day in and day out.

18. Give the audience a brief quiz on your subject either before or after the main part of your speech. You can ask for a show of hands or elicit individual responses from the audience.

19. Divide the audience into small buzz groups and have a reporter from each group share the responses with the whole group. This approach is excellent for use in a workshop type of presentation or when you have been given a very long time for your presentation.

20. Ask the audience for individual responses and write them on a dry-erase board or flip chart. For example, you might ask in a session on public speaking, "What happens to you when you have stage fright?"

21. Pass out a carefully prepared handout—one they will not just sit and read while you're talking. It can be one in which they fill in certain blanks, based on what you're covering. In this way they have a specific task to do during your presentation.

22. Give them group exercises to perform. For example, in a presentation on listening, you could have them divide into pairs and talk to each other at the same time, about their favorite subject, and see how much they learn.

23. Provide opportunities for hands-on practice. For example, in a presentation on letter writing, give them a hypothetical situation and ask them to write a letter based on what you've covered.

24. Physically invade the territory of your audience. Going out into the audience with purpose can really get people involved and make them wonder if you will come to them next.

25. Use audience members to stage an impromptu drama to illustrate your point. For example, a minister had a young man lie down on a bench to portray Isaac on the altar, while he acted out the part of Abraham preparing to kill his son.

26. Take an instant poll of your audience by giving them different colored pieces of cardboard. You could use blue for a positive response and red for a negative answer, for example, or three colors for a multiple-choice question. Ask them to hold up their choice and have assistants tally the response. Then give the audience the results.

27. Before the session, have audience members complete a brief questionnaire about an issue you're addressing. While you are speaking, have an assistant tally the results, and then, near the end of your speech, give the audience the results of their responses. Audience members will be quite interested in knowing how their group thinks about the subject.

28. Hold a question-and-answer session. Tell the audience near the beginning of your speech that you're going to have a Q & A period. This will motivate them to keep track of what you're saying and will give them time to think of a good question on the subject.

Use your imagination to lead your audience to a response. The possibilities are really limitless.

The Use of Humor

Consider: Comedian Bob Hope said, "Humor is the welcome mat between a speaker and his audience. A short joke, a quick laugh, breaks the ice between you and that sea of strangers. When they laugh they're immediately on your side. The laughter makes them your friends. It's the most powerful ammunition you can carry."[20]

The effective use of humor establishes an instant rapport and creates a warm, responsive atmosphere. But dangers lurk therein. Humor must be used judiciously and with caution.

What is humor? Roger P. Wilcox says that humor depends on three elements—incongruity, suddenness, or surprise—followed by a sense of well-being. He goes on to explain that humor occurs when two things which do not normally go together suddenly and unexpectedly are found together and "when somehow we can retain a sense of relative well-being with regard to it."[21]

Alan H. Monroe lists seven different kinds of humor.

1. Exaggeration, overstatement

2. Puns—using words that have a double meaning or which sound like other words with a different meaning

3. Poking fun at dignity or someone in authority

4. Irony—saying something in such a way that the opposite meaning is obviously implied

5. Burlesque—treating absurd things seriously or serious things absurdly

6. Unexpected turns—leading your audience to believe that you are going to say the normal thing and then saying just the opposite

7. Idiosyncrasies of people[22]

Josh McDowell lists several kinds of humor: exaggeration, deliberate understatement, sudden change of thought, surprise thoughts, afterthoughts, the twisting of ideas, misinterpretation of the facts, intentional errors, restatement of a well-known quotation to give it a humorous twist, pantomime, poorly timed gestures, facial grimaces, anecdotes, impersonation of a character, and clever wording.[23]

That description certainly points out the wide diversity of humor, but it's important to realize that humor is far from being an exact science. As author E. B. White quips, humor "can be dissected, as a frog, but the thing dies in the process and the innards are discouraging to any but the pure scientific mind."[24]

Humor creates interest and attention. It makes the speaker appear more human and gets the audience in the speaker's camp. Telling a joke on yourself is a great rapport-builder.

Humor should be relevant to your subject. A humorous story or a joke should move your message forward, not take the audience's attention away from the subject. Don't tell a joke just because you think it's a good story or will get a laugh. What if it doesn't? Then you're stuck in an awkward situation. When a joke that's on the subject doesn't get a laugh, you can always say, "The reason I mentioned that story is…" and continue gracefully on with your speech.

Humor should be in good taste. The bottom line when you tell a joke is not "Did you get a laugh?" but "Did you get a laugh without offending anyone in your audience?" A good rule of thumb to follow is this: "When in doubt, leave it out." Avoid—at all costs—any ethnic jokes or jokes that put down one sex or a group of people—a race, handicapped people, a trade, or a profession.

"LAUGH AND THE WORLD LAUGHS WITH YOU"

A merry heart does good, like medicine,
But a broken spirit dries the bones.
—Proverbs 17:22

Laughter is not at all a bad beginning for a friendship.[15]
—Oscar Wilde

Laughs are therapeutic. They soothe, heal and build relationships,
and give an audience the chance to break the tension of the moment
and draw back to absorb and rethink what you're saying.[16]
—Bob Orben

Wit is a sword; it is meant to make people feel the point
as well as see it.[17]
—G. K. Chesterton

Wit ought to be a glorious treat, like caviar; never spread it about
like marmalade.[18]
—Sir Noel Coward

Laugh at yourself first, before anyone else can.[19]
—Elsa Maxwell

Be sure that the jokes and stories belong to you. No matter what the source, make them your own by adding personal touches, using your own language. Your way of telling a joke or humorous story should match your personality, your style.

Make the story sound as if it really happened—even if it didn't. Telling about your own job interview or about someone's in the audience is more interesting and believable than talking about a faceless blob.

Be aware that receptivity to humor increases as the day goes on. Breakfast is tough. Lunch is OK. Dinner is good. After dinner is best. "People are done with the cares of the day, and they're ready for a laugh," Bob Orben points out.[25]

It is more difficult to get an audience to respond with laughter in an outdoor setting. Laughter is contagious. Things get funnier and funnier as we hear giggles, guffaws, and gales of mirth emanating from those around us. In a setting with good acoustics, the effect is magnified, but outdoor sound is dissipated and diminished. Hearing someone else laugh encourages others to laugh. Hearing laughter also can encourage you as a speaker, get you on "a roll" so that you become funnier and funnier.

Know your audience. You have to know where their heads are. What's their general educational level? How sophisticated or blasé are they? What's their age? What's their general socio-economic level?

Don't try to explain a joke if it falls flat. If it needs explaining, you never should have told it in the first place.

Humor can be used effectively—even if your subject is very serious. In fact, a very heavy topic probably needs the leaven of at least a few smiles or chuckles. Just as a spoonful of sugar helps the medicine go down, a dose of humor can make a controversial or hard message more palatable to the listener. For example, in a sales meeting where sales are down due to an apparent lack of initiative, making a humorous comparison can be much more effective than beating listeners over the head with words of reproach.

Tie humor to major points in your speech. People will often remember a funny story long after they've forgotten the rest. Capitalize on this quality, and let humor help put across your premise and make it memorable.

Sprinkle humor at intervals throughout the speech. There's nothing like a good laugh to keep people alert and awake.

Timing is the critical factor in getting a laugh. Although it seems that some people are just born with a good sense of timing—pausing at the right moment, speeding up, slowing down—most of us have to work to develop that particular skill. And all of us can improve. Study professional comedians, observe how they time their stories, and learn from them.

Too, you don't have to tell jokes successfully to elicit a laugh. Almost all of us can handle a humorous story even if we never seem to get the hang of telling a side-splitting joke. Humor doesn't have to have people doubled over with laughter. Even a quiet smile or a soft chuckle will be enjoyable to your audience.

Also, don't be afraid to ham it up. Acting out a story adds a lot. For instance, if it's a story with two different characters, assume a different stance, facial expression, and body position. For one character, turn slightly to the left; for the other, slightly to the right. Become a thespian. Doing so will add life to your story.

Don't forget to use humor. All of us need its uplifting power. If nothing else, it gives the audience a chance to get together on something. Laughter is a community activity and provides a potent bond with others.

Remember, humor is as essential to a good talk as seasoning is to a good meal. (Also please see the section on the entertaining speech in Chapter 9, page 148)

The Question-and-Answer Session

Consider: Most full-length speeches are not complete without a question-and-answer period.

Many speakers do a superb job of delivering a formal presentation, then ruin the whole thing by poorly handling questions from the audience.

Some Do's

- Treat the question-and-answer period as a part of the speech. The speech is not over until the last question is answered and the speaker sits down.
- Tell the audience at the beginning of your speech that there will be a question-and-answer period.

- It is embarrassing to ask for questions and have none asked because of reluctance on the part of audience members to ask the first question. When this happens, a good technique for "priming the pump" is to say, "A question I am frequently asked is…" and then answer that question. Often that's all that's needed to get the questions flowing.
- Look directly at the person asking the question. Show total interest in that person and what is being asked.
- Listen for both content and feeling by observing facial expressions and body language.
- Repeat the question for the rest of the audience in case some did not hear it.
- If you're not sure exactly what the questioner means, paraphrase the question by saying, "Let me be sure I understand what you're asking."
- Thank the questioner. Look at the entire audience while answering, glancing back occasionally at the person who asked the question.
- If the question is emotionally charged or belligerent, show understanding of the person's position or feelings. Demonstrate that you value the questioner as a person even though your position may be quite different. Never put down the questioner or engage in a verbal battle.
- Treat two questions from the same person as two separate questions.
- Admit you don't have an answer if you don't know. Offer to find out and get back to that person. Ask for the questioner's name and phone number and be sure to contact him or her later.
- Be factual and accurate. Avoid phrases such as, "They say…" or "A recent report…" or "It is a well-known fact…"
- Rotate the way you select questions from the audience. Let individuals seated in all areas of the room have a chance to speak.
- Anticipate the kinds of questions you will be asked and have statistics or quotations at your fingertips.
- Maintain a positive attitude. Avoid getting on the defensive.
- Remain in control of the session.
- Do not let the question-and-answer session drag on or fizzle out. Be sure to keep it within the time limits set by the program

chairman. When you're nearly out of time, tell your audience, "There's time for only one more question."

- Keep your answers to the point, but be sure to answer the question as completely as possible. A good format to follow in many cases is to give a one-sentence answer or a "yes" or "no," give the reason, a brief example, and a restatement of your answer.
- Turn a complaint or non-question into a question. For example, if a member of the audience says, "We sure don't need any higher taxes," you might say, "I hear a very important question in your statement. Why should we pay any more taxes than we're already paying?" Then answer the question you made up.
- Save a clincher statement, a summary of your speech, or a dynamic ending to use at the end of your question-and-answer session rather than just trailing off after the last question and mumbling "thank you."

Some Don'ts

- Resist the temptation to gather up your notes and prepare to leave the speaker's stand while the first question is being asked. Doing this makes the speaker appear to be not really interested in answering questions the audience might have.
- Don't grade questions by telling one questioner, "That's a good question," but not telling others their questions are good, too. Just answer the question.
- Don't allow one or two persons to ask all the questions. Simply say, "Many others have questions. I'll get back to you if there is time."
- Avoid answering with such phrases as "Well, obviously…" or "As I said in my speech…" or "Anyone should know the answer to that.…" These are all put-down phrases and make potential participants hesitant to ask questions.
- Don't use negative body language. Avoid putting your hands on your hips or folding your arms over your chest while you're listening to the question or answering.
- Don't point one finger at your audience while speaking. That's a scolding pose and would make you seem "preachy."
- Avoid "off-the-record" statements.
- Never hedge or avoid answering a question. Give the audience a straight answer.
- Don't argue with the questioner. If he or she persists, offer to discuss the question with the person after the meeting.

- Don't get down on the level of a nasty questioner. Usually the audience will take care of a rude member in its midst if you remain the "good guy."
- Don't feel obligated to agree with the questioner if you actually disagree, but learn to disagree diplomatically.

Audience Connection—Worth the Effort

Taking the time and effort to search out everything you can about your audience and finding ways to involve them in your presentation pay big dividends in making your speech successful, meaningful, and full of impact. Even though you may be the proverbial "silver tongued orator," without that investment into learning your audience your words will be like the "sounding brass or tinkling cymbal" (1 Cor. 13: 1). Paying attention to detail and making the effort to truly communicate with your listener does demonstrate that you care about her or him.

A critically important question to ask yourself is this: "Who is the target for my words?" If your answer is a group of 50, 100, or 500 people, then you could use an adjustment to your thinking. Never lose sight of the fact that you are speaking to one person, regardless of how many individuals are present, rather than a faceless blob of people.

One successful speaker says he likes to think of a member of his audience as a friend sitting across from him at his kitchen table. Periodically he imagines the friend asking, "Why are you telling me this? What has that to do with me?" He says that maintaining that mental image and posing those kinds of questions help him to make his remarks relate more effectively to his listener's life and needs. He also believes that practice helps keep his style of speaking more intimate and less pompous.

Charles Templeton made this point well with the following anecdote: "Many years ago in Indianapolis, an old preacher asked why I was so tense. 'Because,' I replied, 'there are 5000 people out there expecting me to be helpful.' 'No, there aren't,' he said. 'There's only one person, Charles. No one hears you as a crowd. Everyone hears you as an individual.'"[26]

Remember what Aristotle said: "Of the three elements in speech making—speaker, subject, and persons addressed—it is the last one, the hearer, that determines the speech's end and object."

Chapter 6

SHOW AND TELL YOUR MESSAGE

The hearing ear and the seeing eye,
The Lord has made them both (Prov. 20:12).

Write my answer on a billboard, large and clear, so that
anyone can read it at a glance and rush to tell the others.
Hab. 2:2 (LB)

Consider: "When relying on verbalization alone to communicate, an estimated 90 percent of a message is misinterpreted or forgotten entirely. We retain only 10 percent of what we hear. Adding appropriate visual aids to verbalization increases retention to approximately 50 percent."[1]

Biblical Accounts of Audiovisual Approaches

The use of audiovisual approaches in communicating is certainly no new thing.

In fact, the Bible is filled with dramatic usage of audiovisuals:

- The burning bush Moses saw in the desert
- Moses' staff that turned into a snake and then back again into a staff
- The ten commandments written on tablets of stone
- The ladder in Jacob's dream, with angels ascending and descending
- The bronze serpent God commanded Moses to make in the wilderness
- The rainbow after the Flood
- The star over the stable in Bethlehem where Jesus was born

- The dove that descended when John the Baptist baptized Jesus in the River Jordan
- The tongues of fire and the rushing wind on the Day of Pentecost

Apparently God understood and used the power of sight and sound in communicating with men and women.

Jesus also understood the power of involving His listeners' senses so that His message would be noted, remembered, and understood.

What a dramatic, audiovisual scene! Jesus, whip in hand, amid the clang of the coins, crashing tables, and bleating sheep and cattle. The purpose of the temple had been corrupted, not by those who bought and sold animals, but by religious leaders with their self-serving and exclusiveness. Jesus got the attention of the crowd, made His point, and accomplished His purpose (Matt. 21:12-13).

He continued to use creative audiovisual approaches throughout His ministry. Some examples of these approaches are these:

- He rode on a donkey for his entry into Jerusalem (Luke 19:29-36).
- He washed the feet of his disciples, using a towel and washbasin of water, as an example of servanthood (John 13:4-17).
- He slept during the storm on the Sea of Galilee and then dramatically rebuked the wind and the waves, causing a dead calm in the turbulent waters (Matt. 9:23-27).

One of the most powerful uses of audiovisuals was Jesus' final meal with His disciples. That last supper was full of real objects with symbolic meaning. In the typical order of the festal meal, all the senses were involved. Many items were strongly visual. The participants heard the prayers and interpretation for each of the parts of the meal. Several distinct aromas emanated from the various items of food. The sense of touch was involved as the vegetable was dipped into the bowl of salt and the bread was handled. Various flavors were tasted as the participants ate each of the symbolic elements.

At this Last Supper, Jesus took symbolic, visual elements and gave them new meaning. For His disciples, partaking of the bread and cup at the Last Supper made a lasting sensory impression (Luke 22: 14-20), and it continues to create a vivid experience for Christians.

Jesus used simple, but highly creative sensory approaches in communicating His message, with stunning results. We would do well to follow His example—especially in light of the fact that our culture is virtually immersed in sensory experiences. The impact of television and other media is something speakers cannot afford to ignore. Without compromising our message, we can capitalize on the heightened impact of, and familiarity with, multi-media approaches so prevalent in today's society. The immersion of our culture in images has resulted in a greater dependency on sight for learning, attention-keeping, and stimulation.

Contemporary Usage of Audiovisuals

Contemporary practitioners affirm this approach. The Bell and Howell Corporation offered these statistics: people learn eighty-three percent by sight, eleven percent by hearing, three-and-a-half percent by smell, one-and-a-half percent by touch, and one percent by taste.[2]

In an experiment on communication, the Mobil Oil Company found the following: After three days, only ten percent of the material taught by simple telling could be recalled. Twenty percent of the material that had only been shown was remembered, but an impressive sixty-five percent of the material taught by both telling and showing was retained.[3]

Technology has ushered in a whole host of approaches that can be used effectively to add life and longevity to the speaker's words. In fact, there are so many choices that sorting through them can get confusing. Knowing which aid to use where and in what circumstances and using the aid effectively are vitally important. In fact, audiovisual usage can be distracting and detrimental to your message when the following are true:

- Visual material contains a lot of print or detail too small to be seen.
- Sound is distorted, too soft to be easily heard, or excruciatingly loud.
- Equipment is not working properly or is not operated correctly.

Here are some guidelines to keep in mind when using audiovisuals:

1. Remember the three B's. Visual materials must be

Big
   Bold
      Brilliant

2. A good visual standard to use is this:
   - One idea per visual
   - Six words per line
   - Six lines per visual

3. Visual material should be simple. A common mistake is trying to put too much information on each visual.

4. Although visual material can provide reinforcement, variety, and interest, monotony can result if the same approach is used repeatedly.

5. Check the equipment and make sure it is working properly well in advance of the meeting.

6. If a screen or monitor is to be used, make sure it is located where everyone can easily see it.

7. Check the volume level on audio equipment and set it properly in advance. A deafening roar at the beginning or an inaudible first minute of a presentation negates much of the potential benefit.

8. If lights need to be turned off and then back on, assign someone to carry out that very important task. Work out in advance all necessary cues with others who are assisting with or participating in the presentation.

9. Have someone check all audiovisual material for errors and for clarity of meaning. Be sure that any material used is sharp-looking. A sloppy visual makes a poor impression and should be redone or scratched from the presentation.

10. Practice the presentation if there are several pieces to manipulate. If more than one person is involved, have a rehearsal beforehand to make sure everything is working properly and everyone understands what to do.

11. Place any aids that the speaker will use near the speaker's stand or position. Avoid long treks back and forth from equipment or a dry-erase board.

12. Check any tendency to speak toward a visual aid. Always be sure to face the audience.

13. Don't block the audience's view of the visual.

14. Keep the visual up long enough for the viewer to grasp its message. Doing this is especially important if participants are taking notes.

15. Remember to interact with the group while using audiovisual approaches. Although interaction is not possible with some media, such as a film, other aids lend themselves beautifully to audience involvement.

Audiovisual material is aptly called an aid. It should be used to help you communicate more effectively—not do your job for you. Do not let your audiovisual aids overpower you. Remember, you're still the star of the show. You should not be upstaged.

The information contained on the next few pages should help you in deciding on the most appropriate approach for your particular presentation.

Computer-Controlled Presentations

The advent of the computer has brought an amazingly effective resource into the world of audiovisual production. In fact, in recent years, it has become the star approach for the speaker who wants to communicate effectively, keep the audience's attention, give a professional-appearing presentation, and make a cutting-edge contemporary impression on his or her audience.

Jeff Burger, a consultant and prolific author on multimedia, says, "There are several major compelling reasons for making the leap to computer-controlled presentations—malleability, cost-saving, and impact."[6] Some of the flexibility aspects that he points out are the ability to re-sort slides with a few mouse clicks rather than having to empty a slide carousel and reposition slides by hand; being able to put together a presentation at the last minute;

easily restructuring a presentation for various audiences; and being able to use a master template to change the background font or color scheme of a presentation to appeal to audiences according to gender, age, or ethnic background.[7]

Software packages such as Microsoft PowerPoint, Astound, Freelance Graphics, and SPC's Harvard Graphics make it possible to execute a presentation directly from the computer. This approach eliminates the considerable expense and time constraints of a slide production. Another advantage is that existing elements, such as printed materials and other media, may be used easily.[8]

Advantages:
- Many set-ups can utilize video sources and graphics with a single screen.
- Animation and digital video add interest with effects such as charts growing over a period of time and text and images flying into place.
- Direct support for audio files ensures synchronization with visual material.
- Once developed, the material is simple to use.

Disadvantage:
- Computers can crash, resulting in having to reboot the computer, take other corrective measures, or be left holding the bag.

Tips:
- It is strongly recommended that the computer-generated presentation be transferred to a CD or DVD as a backup. This provides protection of your work in case of a computer crash and portability for use on any appropriate projector. However, if the presentation is going to be made using a computer, use the same computer on which the material was developed to deliver the presentation, since variations from computer to computer can cause unforeseen problems.

- Audience size must be taken into consideration. A standard-sized computer monitor is effective only with a very small group of people. Monitors from 25 to 40 inches may be used successfully with a moderately sized audience. For larger audiences, using a projection system or renting one with specific capabilities is advisable. Transparent LCD panels that fit on overhead projectors with at least 4,000 lumens for proper brightness, contrast, and color fidelity can also be used effectively. A standard overhead projector will not work. It is necessary to rent or buy a superbright one. LCD projectors are also available. They are less cumbersome to use than the LCD panel with an overhead projector, and they are growing in popularity.

Audiovisual Aid: Overhead Projector

One of the most versatile aids and an easy one to use, particularly in a teaching situation, is the overhead projector. However, you don't want to overdo it. Arriving at the lectern with a foot-high stack of overhead transparencies can elicit internal groans, or more, from a group.

Advantages:
- Transparencies can be used in a lighted room.
- Transparencies can be used with a rather large group of people.
- The speaker can operate the projector and thus maintain complete control over the presentation.
- The speaker can face the audience and does not have to leave the speaking area.
- The speaker can point out features on the transparency, with a pen, on the stage of the projector itself.
- Transparencies can be used periodically during the presentation by merely flipping on a switch.
- Prepared transparencies can be used to reveal the information a line at a time when this is desirable.
- Information on a prepared transparency can be highlighted with a special pen during the presentation.
- The presenter can write on the transparency during the presentation. Feedback from the audience can easily be recorded and projected for the whole group to see and consider.
- Transparencies are relatively inexpensive.
- Professional-looking transparencies can be made using a large font on a computer and a copying machine—equipment that's usually easily accessible.

- Overhead projectors can be equipped with a two-way acetate roll attachment allowing the speaker to use a continuous roll of acetate when this would be easier.

Disadvantages:
- A keystone effect of the image will result unless projector and screen are carefully positioned.

Tips:
- The screen should be positioned at an angle behind and to the left or right of the speaker. Otherwise, the view of the listener will be blocked.
- Color-highlight film can be used to good effect on portions of the transparency.
- Overlays can be effectively used in showing the parts of a whole.
- Opaque background film gives a dramatic effect since it looks as if the writing or drawing suddenly appeared.
- The projector should be turned off when you're through making your point; otherwise, the old information is distracting.
- Mount transparencies in frames for easy handling and number the frames in order of presentation. Simple notes may also be written on the frame.
- Beware of using the same repetitious pattern for too long a period. It's a good idea to vary your presentation. For example, you might use two or three transparencies revealing a point at a time, then a transparency making a single point. Using transparencies throughout an entire presentation can become monotonous.

Audiovisual Aid: Models and Objects

Real objects are highly effective in getting persons curious about what on earth you are going to do with that thing. Real objects pique the audience's interest in your topic, draw them into your discussion, keeping them interested, and focus their attention.

The use of objects is not for children only. Paul Avery reinforced that theory with his use of puppets at Meadowcreek Community Church in Mesquite, Texas. "The power of puppetry is cheapened when we use it with children only," he said. He found that adults, as much as children, enjoy and are intrigued by puppets. He told of an inspiration he had to use Banruki puppetry, a Japanese form in which life-size puppets are used, with the puppeteers, dressed in black, in full view of the audience—in a Christmas service. The huge puppets depicted Mary and Joseph. He recalled that many people were weeping. Evidently the unconventional approach to telling an old, familiar story lent a new dimension and made it come to life through the use of inanimate objects.[4]

Advantages:
- Models and objects are good attention getters and can add realism to a presentation.
- Visual aids that actually do something during the speech are especially interesting.
- The three-dimensional aspect gives them a distinct advantage over pictures.
- Models and objects can usually be handled by the audience, giving a kinesthetic dimension to the presentation.

Disadvantage:
- Models and objects cannot be used effectively with a large group unless they are very big.

Tips:
- The object or model should be concealed until the time for its discussion in your presentation. Otherwise, it will be distracting.
- If it is impossible to let everyone in the group manipulate the object or model during the presentation, provide an opportunity for the others after you are finished.
- Be sure the object or model is positioned high enough so that those seated on the back row will be able to see it.
- Even something too small to be seen can be used effectively if you want to show just how small it really is.
- Let your imagination run riot in coming up with ideas for the use of real-life objects. For example, a former secretary of agriculture used slices from a real loaf of bread to show the percentage of profit that the farmer, the baker, and the retailer receive.

Audiovisual Aid: Sound

Sound can be used effectively in a number of ways within a presentation. Its use is limited only by your imagination.

Advantages:
- A speaker can back up a point of view with the voice of an expert on the subject or a main player in a dramatic situation.
- Pre-recorded voices may be used to dramatize a point. For example, in speaking of the baptism of Jesus, you could arrange to have a deep voice, recorded with an echo effect, say, "This is my Son, the Beloved, with whom I am well pleased" (Matthew 3:17).
- Recorded or actual sounds may be used to illustrate or dramatize a point.
- Live or recorded music can be used effectively to set the mood for a particular presentation, or to change the emotional climate during a presentation.
- A live telephone conversation with someone, such as a missionary in another country, can be set up and take place during a presentation. A speaker phone and use of the public address system can enable everyone to hear both sides of the conversation. A visual presentation can be added to enhance the value of the conversation.
- Sound can be used effectively to involve participants in a lesson.
- The tape recorder may be used effectively in training when the spoken word is important.

Disadvantages:
- Care must be taken that all audience members can hear the recording.
- If the recording is very long, the audience may lose interest with nothing to watch.

Tip:
- Don't overlook the audio recorder as a possibility to add color and life to your presentation.

Audiovisual Aid: Slide Projector

Slides can be used effectively in a number of ways within a presentation.

Advantages:
- Slides are effective with a large audience.
- With a carousel projector and remote control, the speaker can operate the equipment.

- The speaker can dwell as long as desired on one particular slide.
- Slide presentations can be easily changed and varied according to the interest of the audience and the appropriateness of the occasion.
- Visual material related to the points of a message may be shown at the appropriate time to help the audience stay focused.
- Words of a poem or a song may be projected onto the screen. Caution: be sure that copyright laws are not infringed.
- Key phrases you may want the audience to repeat may appear on the screen.
- Pictures of key persons and places in your presentation can be shown. For example, if you're talking about outstanding ministers of the past, consider having slides made of pictures of St. Francis of Assisi or John Wesley instead of just telling about them.
- Pictures of paintings and other works of art may be shown.
- Announcements of interest to the group may be projected before the meeting or service begins.

Disadvantage:
- Overhead lighting must be subdued.

Tips:
- It is best to limit the length of the slide show to ten to fifteen minutes.
- Cardboard frames on slides are safer than plastic ones, which will sometimes warp when they get hot in the projector.
- The speaker should stand to the right of the screen (audience's left). Since we read from left to right, this is a stronger position for maintaining audience attention.
- A light on the lectern will be needed if the speaker must use notes during the slide presentation.
- A cordless remote slide changer may be purchased, which gives the speaker a great deal more freedom of movement.
- Pace the slide show to maintain audience interest. Keeping one slide on the screen too long invites audience members' minds to drift. As a rule, six to eight slides per minute will maintain attention.

- Don't give in to the temptation to use a nearly good slide. Select only those that are of top quality and have something to say.
- Check to be sure the slides are loaded properly. An upside down shot or one with the letters running backwards puts a damper on the whole presentation.

Audiovisual Aid: Movies

A wide variety of subject matter is available on film. Besides those specifically made on religious topics, excerpts from commercial sources may be used effectively to set up a topic as a launching pad or illustration for a lesson, sermon, or discussion. Speakers wishing to use this approach should be aware of the legal requirements.[5]

Advantages:
- Films can show movement.
- The audience can be vicariously transported to another location, another time in history.
- Watching a film or an excerpt can provide a common experience for the audience.
- The film can serve as a launching pad for discussion.
- Many types of films are available for rental or for purchase at varying costs.
- Films may be shown to a very large group of people although additional speakers may be necessary in a large auditorium.

Disadvantages:
- The room must be darkened.
- A professional projectionist is necessary.
- The speaker loses rapport with the audience since, as a rule, the film or video is self-contained, and the speaker cannot interact.

Tips:
- Projectors should never be left to run alone.
- The film should be carefully introduced to prepare the viewer for what is important or of particular interest to the group.
- Highlights of the film should be summarized afterwards.
- The film may be used as an excellent vehicle to launch a group discussion.

Audiovisual Aid: Television

Although television has many of the same advantages of film, it has some additional plusses as well as some minuses.

Advantages:
- Television can be used in a lighted room.
- Many videocassette tapes and DVDs on a variety of subjects are available at a reasonable price. Again, be certain to comply with copyright laws.
- Equipment can be easily stopped and started to call attention to a certain point.
- Television is particularly helpful in training situations, such as public speaking and sales, since feedback can be immediate.
- Material may be edited with proper equipment.
- Television shows motion and is good for demonstrations and for showing up close an object the audience could not otherwise see.

Disadvantage:
- Television cannot be effectively used with a large group of people unless a very large screen is rented. This runs several hundred dollars for rental and is available only in larger cities.

Tip:
- If you have a good-sized audience, use more than one receiver, located for optimum viewing.

Audiovisual Aid: Dry-Erase Board

Certainly one of the oldest, but still effective audiovisual aids is the chalkboard or, in much greater use today, the dry-erase board.

Advantages:
- Key points and words can be easily and spontaneously emphasized.
- Responses from the audience can be listed and referred to.
- Material can be erased and the board reused immediately.

Disadvantages:

- Dry-erase boards cannot be used effectively with a large group.
- The audience's attention may be easily lost as the speaker writes with his or her back to the audience.
- Dry-erase boards are difficult to position so that the entire group can readily see them.

Tips:

- Be sure the writing is large enough to be easily read from the back row. With a viewing distance from the dry-erase board of thirty-two feet, lettering should be at least two-and-a-half inches high.
- Limit your writing to key words or phrases.
- While you write, do not remain with your back to the audience for more than a few seconds at a time.
- If information is written in advance of the presentation, be sure the dry-erase board is turned around or covered. Otherwise, the audience will read instead of listening to the speaker.
- Because of the contrast, a black marker is more readable than a colored one.
- Once you have written on the dry-erase board, get away from it. Doing this is important so that you don't block the audience's view and also so that you don't succumb to the temptation to "fiddle" with the board.
- Use a pointer rather than your hand if you wish to emphasize certain written information.
- Erase the dry-erase board when you are finished using it. Otherwise, the written information will be distracting.
- Erase writing immediately after the presentation. Otherwise, writing will become difficult to remove.
- Be sure to use only markers made for dry-erase boards. Permanent markers have ruined many dry-erase boards, permantly.
- Dry-erase boards need to be cleaned periodically with a special cleaning fluid.

Audiovisual Aid: Flip Chart

Another oldie but goodie is the flip chart. It is particularly effective for use in developing a plan of action and involving the group.

Advantages:
- Flip charts are relatively inexpensive.
- Material can be prepared in advance, using color in drawings, graphs, and charts.
- Key points and words can be easily and spontaneously emphasized.
- Responses from audience members can be listed and referred to.

Disadvantages:
- Flip charts cannot be used effectively with a large group.
- It is easy to lose your audience's attention if you write with your back to the audience for too long a period of time.

Tips:
- Use a blank sheet as you begin your presentation.
- Place blank sheets between pre-prepared sheets so that you may cover your message when you are speaking on a different subject.
- Be sure the writing is large enough (and thick enough) to be easily read from the back row.
- Limit your writing to key words or phrases.
- While you write, do not remain with your back to the audience for more than a few seconds at a time.
- Practice turning the sheets until it becomes easy and second nature.
- Once you have written on the sheet or turned to the next page, move away from the chart.
- Use a pointer rather than your hand if you wish to emphasize certain written information or a part of a chart or graph.
- Be sure not to block the view of the audience.
- If you prepare charts in advance, have someone else proof them for errors.
- Know the material on your charts so you don't have to read from them and end up with a swivel head from looking back and forth at them and at your audience.

Audiovisual Aid: Flannel, Hook-and-Loop, and Magnet Boards

The flannel board has been used throughout the years. Hook-and-loop and magnet boards are more recent entries that serve much the same purpose.

Advantages
- Drawings or work of the group may be easily displayed.
- Materials such as cloth, yarn, bits of balsa wood, blotting paper, and sponge will adhere to a flannel board. Hook-and-loop boards allow objects to be firmly attached yet instantly removed or manipulated. Odd-shaped and heavy objects (up to several pounds) may also be attached. Small metal objects will adhere to a magnet board and magnets may be used to hold thin objects of paper or cloth.
- An idea presentation may be built, piece by piece, in an orderly sequence.
- Members of the audience may be involved by the speaker's asking them to regroup or reposition the objects for a specific reason.
- These boards may be used effectively in teaching a group how to play a particular sport, game, or skill. They may also add interest to the telling of a story.

Disadvantage:
- Magnet, hook-and-loop, and flannel boards cannot be used effectively with a large group.

Tips:
- Presentations with magnet, hook-and-loop, and flannel boards should be kept simple.
- A flannel board should be tilted back very slightly at the top to help materials stick firmly to the flannel surface.
- Be sure to step aside after applying the picture or object to the board's surface so as not to block the audience's line of vision.
- Have a conveniently close working surface available to store visual material before and after use.
- Check the order of visual material and be sure it is separated for easy handling.

Audiovisual Aid: Microphone

Many improvements in microphone technology in recent years have assisted voice enhancement to a marked degree.

Advantages:
- The voice can be amplified to ensure audibility.
- A lavaliere microphone gives the speaker greater flexibility, and a cordless mike provides the maximum ease of movement.

- In a relatively large area, the speaker can speak very softly for effect without worrying about being heard.

Disadvantages:
- Unless excellent equipment is available, the voice can be distorted.
- Use of a stationary mike limits the movement of speaker.
- A hand-held mike limits the effectiveness of gestures.
- Microphones magnify speech defects, such as a hissing sound or smacking of lips.
- Feedback can be very disconcerting to an audience. Correct positioning and operation are essential.

Tips:
- Speaker should try out the mike before the meeting begins and set the level appropriately. Realize that a full auditorium will change the sound, and the level will probably need to be adjusted.
- Speaker should be certain to know how to turn the mike on and adjust the height of the stand.
- Speaker must be adept at using a mike effectively—backing away when getting louder and getting closer when softer.
- Speaker must realize that she or he cannot really tell how the voice sounds to the audience and must rely on the sound technician to make necessary adjustments.
- Speaker should not substitute the use of a microphone for good projection techniques.
- Speaker must be aware that feedback can result if the mike is placed too close to other sound equipment such as speakers and other microphones.

Audiovisual Aid: Handouts
A well-prepared handout can be a real asset to a presentation.

Advantages:
- Handouts can involve listeners in the presentation by giving them a certain graph or chart to look at or a quiz to take.
- Handouts can reinforce the presentation later and can be valuable for future reference.
- Information about the speaker and the presentation on the handout can lead to other speaking engagements.

Disadvantage:
- Handouts can become so absorbing to the audience that it may be difficult for the speaker to keep members' attention.

Tips:
- Be sure to make arrangements with enough helpers to get the material handed out quickly, quietly, and efficiently.
- Be certain to have more than enough copies available for those present. Audience members become very irritated if they don't get a handout—even if they don't particularly want one.
- If the handout is the same as your presentation, do not hand it out until after the presentation. Above all, don't stand up and read the handout aloud to your audience.
- Unless following the handout is important to your presentation, wait until after you finish to distribute it. Otherwise, people have a tendency to sit and read instead of listening to what you're saying.
- If you prepare the material yourself, be sure to have someone else proof the final copy.
- Make sure the reproduction is of top quality. A barely legible or ink-smeared copy makes a negative statement about you as a speaker.
- Handout materials should have the name of the material and the speaker's or author's name on each page.
- If the material is original, place the copyright symbol or "copyright" by your name and the date on the handout.
- Copyrighted material should not be included in a handout without permission.

Audiovisual approaches are limited only by our imaginations. And they are certainly worth the extra time and effort required in terms of making your presentation more interesting and memorable.

AUDIOVISUAL CHECKLIST

❑ Have you checked out the meeting room or the auditorium to be sure of any necessary adaptive measures and their availability, such as use of extension cords, means of darkening the room, or special stands?

❑ Have you allowed plenty of time for setting up and testing audiovisual equipment?

❑ Have you checked several days in advance of the engagement to be certain all equipment is in good working order?

❑ Do you have the equipment in place and in the most advantageous position?

❑ Have you placed electrician's tape over any extension cords where people may be walking?

❑ Have you focused any projectors you may be using?

❑ Have you cued up any tapes or films so that there will be no awkward pause when they are turned on?

❑ Have you made arrangements with someone to turn off and on the lights (if necessary) on a certain cue?

❑ Have you concealed any audiovisual material so that it will be easy to unmask at the appropriate time?

❑ Have you tested the level of any sound equipment you plan to use, including a microphone?

❑ Have you checked out the visibility of your material from all parts of the meeting area?

❑ Have you made arrangements with a competent projectionist to turn on and off the equipment on cue and make certain it is working properly if you cannot operate it yourself?

❑ Do you have spare bulbs on hand in case the one in your projector burns out?

❑ Do you have your slides, transparencies, or other material numbered, and have you checked to make sure they are in the proper order?

Chapter 7

WRITING THE SPEECH

For precept must be upon precept, precept upon precept,
Line upon line, line upon line,
Here a little, there a little (Isaiah 28:10).

Keep It Simple, Speaker

There's an old formula, the KISS formula, that public speakers would profit from taking to heart,...and that is to keep it simple.

An acquaintance once asked Abraham Lincoln how he managed to have his unusual ability of "putting things" when he spoke. Lincoln replied, in part,

> Among my earliest recollections, I remember how when a mere child, I used to get irritated when anybody talked to me in a way I couldn't understand. I don't think I ever got angrier at anything else in my life.

> I can remember going to my little bedroom after hearing the neighbors talk of an evening, with my father, and spending no small part of the night walking up and down and trying to make out the exact meaning of some of their, to me, dark sayings. I could not sleep, though I often tried to, when I got in such a hunt after an idea, until I caught it; and when I thought I had got it, I was still not satisfied until I had repeated it over and over, until I put it in language plain enough, as I thought, for any boy I knew to comprehend.

> This was a kind of passion with me, and it has stuck, for I am never easy now, when I am handling a thought, till I have bounded it north and bounded it south, and bounded it east and bounded it west. Perhaps that accounts for the characteristics you observe in my speeches, though I never put the two things together before.[1]

Speakers also would do well to heed an old country preacher's formula for a good sermon.

The preacher had an unusual knack for delivering sermons that people actually remembered until the next Sunday, and even beyond. He was asked, "How do you do it? I find myself thinking about what you said all week, when usually I can't remember past Sunday dinner what a sermon was about." The preacher replied, "It's really quite simple. I just tell them what I'm going to tell them. I tell them. Then I tell them what I told them."

He used repetition to help the congregation stay on track and remember what he said.

In the beginning grab their interest.
In the middle expand their understanding.
In the end reinforce and cap it off.

Like a gamefish, a speech needs:

a head...
a connecting spine with plenty of muscular support...
and a tail.²

Consider: Some years ago the British House of Commons was interrupted by the news that the cable to Africa had been completed. After the huzzahs and hat-tossing had died down, Winston Churchill rose to say, "Excellent. Excellent. Now, what shall we tell the Africans?"[3]

You've been asked to speak. You've accepted. Now, what will you tell your audience?

Other vital questions include these:

- How can you get their attention?
- How can you keep them listening?
- How can you help them remember what they have heard?

Someone has said that "an agreement to make a speech may be compared with a pregnancy. Only as the day of delivery draws near does the full realization of the magnitude of your commitment to deliver hit you."

As a speaker, sometimes you will be given a specific topic or a general subject to speak on. Other times you will be told to talk about whatever you want to. Regardless of which option you are given, it will be up to you to determine exactly what approach you will take, just how broad or narrow to make the subject, and how you will make it specifically apply to and interest the audience you will be addressing.

The Objective of Your Speech

A top priority for you as a speaker is to decide your purpose for making this particular speech. What do you hope to do for (or to) your audience? There are six main objectives a speaker may adopt for a presentation.

1. To stimulate the audience, to persuade them to a particular point of view at an emotional level.

2. To convince the listeners, to convey truth through a factual, logical approach.

3. To actuate the hearers, to get them to make a commitment to take action.

4. To inform the audience by presenting facts from an unbiased viewpoint.

5. To entertain the crowd in a non-persuasive, light-hearted presentation.

6. To inspire the listeners to a broader perspective, a more humanitarian viewpoint, a nobler purpose.

You may have only one of those objectives or you may combine more than one objective. For example, your purpose may include persuading your audience to adopt a certain viewpoint and then motivating them to move on a certain course of action.

Once you have determined your purpose, then the question is how do you prepare the material for a speech? Where do you begin? How do you go about constructing an interesting, attention-keeping presentation?

The Five Basic Parts of a Speech

In putting together your speech, it will serve you well to keep in mind the five basic parts of a speech:

1. *Title:* a brief statement that says in a nutshell what the presentation is about. The title needs to be interest-piquing and an accurate description of your topic.

2. *Introduction:* your first, and often only, chance to grab the listener's attention and interest.

3. *Statement of purpose:* a short synopsis of what the presentation is about and what the listener will gain from hearing it.

4. *Body:* the substance of the presentation, usually containing not more than three to five main points.

5. *Conclusion:* a short summary of the main points, with a zinger end statement for the listener to take away.

Or put another way in keeping with the advice of the old country preacher,

- We use the title and introduction to garner interest.
- We use the statement of purpose to tell them what we are going to tell them.
- We use the body to tell them.
- And we use the conclusion to tell them what we have told them.

Effective Titles

The choice of a title for a presentation can be highly significant. An effective title announced ahead of time may motivate listeners to think to themselves: "That sounds interesting. I want to hear that speaker." By contrast, an ineffective title may be de-motivating and have a negative effect on attendance.

Here are some pointed questions to ask about titles:

1. Does it get your attention? Does it pique your curiosity? Walden Books says that sixty-five percent of the people who pick up a book at a bookstore will buy it. The title is a major reason someone picks up a book or decides whether or not to read an article. The title may also be a major

reason for some in deciding whether they come to hear your speech (or stay away).

2. Does it fit the subject matter? Does it describe your subject? After all, you do not want to be charged with false advertising.

3. Does it match the tone of your message and your approach as a speaker? You do not want to use a flippant title with a very serious subject or approach, or vice versa.

4. Does it make the reader wonder, or does it tell too much?

5. Does it alienate part of the group? Are the words too feminine, too masculine, too young, or too dated for the projected listeners?

6. Is it compelling? Picture Allen, who is dead tired from working two jobs so he can keep up his child support payments, or Ellen, who has been up half the night with a baby with the colic. Will your title motivate them to hop out of bed and rush out, or will they say, "So what?" and turn back over for a few more winks of sleep?

7. Who is your targeted audience? What are their interests? What is their vocabulary? Use terms that connect with their world.

Here are some suggestions.

- Keep your title short, four or five words at the most. Consider how it will look in a program, a flyer, or on the sign out front.
- Toy with words and try to come up with something that has a nice "ring" to it. Consider alliteration or a play on words.
- Say the title aloud and see how it sounds when spoken. Does it have a flow, an interesting rhythm?
- Bounce possibilities off friends and colleagues whose opinions you trust. Watch their reaction as well as their verbal response. You will be able to tell if you have captured their interest.
- Think of the title as a terse summary or the essence of your entire presentation. Get to the heart of the matter.
- Use the title of your presentation to provide continuity in the body of the presentation and to remind your listeners of

your subject. For example, in a presentation for seniors titled "Sarah and Abraham Didn't Retire," after each point you could say, "Remember! Sarah and Abraham didn't retire."

- Consider using a question. A provocative question automatically sparks involvement by challenging the listener to come up with an answer.

Here are some different types of titles.

- Reversal: "Are the Heavenly Minded Any Earthly Good?" "When You Do It Right and It Turns Out Wrong"
- How to: "Five Ways to Win Over Worry"
- Negative: "Jesus Dallied 'Til Lazarus Died"
- Rhyme: "Winning the Race with Grace," "The Age of Rage"
- Pun: "Rising to the Occasion" (an Easter sermon)
- Repetition: "The Duties of the Day Performed in the Day"
- Paradox: "How to Gain Your Life by Losing It"
- Alliteration: "The Genius of Gentleness," "The Righteous and Their Reward"
- Surprise: "Family Ties That Bind and Gag"
- Play on words: "State of the Union" (a series on marriage)
- Appeal to well-being: "The Present Obscurity and Future Glory of the Righteous"
- Humor: "Honey, I Shrunk the Devil"
- Contrast: "Great Results from Small Beginnings," "The Proud Abased; the Humble Exalted"
- Parody on a saying: "The Lies that Bind," "Don't Fall Back, Step Up" (the Sunday Daylight Saving Time ends), "When the End Doesn't Justify the Means"
- Quotation: "I've Never Seen the Righteous Forsaken"
- Current slogan or saying: "You Deserve a Break Today" "God Cared Enough to Send the Very Best"
- Question: "What Would Jesus Say to Madonna?" "Did the Devil Make Me Do It?"

Naming anything is challenging—whether it is a child, a church, or a message. But a name is important, even critical, to its success.

The Introduction

The first words of your presentation are the most important you will utter. They may well determine whether anyone will listen to the rest of your remarks. Research studies have shown that you have only the first four minutes to prove yourself as a speaker. During that time, listeners will make an important decision: Is your message going to be worth hearing? If the answer is "no," then they probably will become present in the body but absent in the mind as they plan next summer's vacation or decide where to go for dinner after the meeting.

Laurie Rozakis has an interesting way of looking at opening remarks. "You can't go wrong if you think of the first two minutes of your speech as an audition. It's a 120-second sample that has to convince your listeners that the remaining 20 minutes are worth their time and attention."[4]

Because the first words are so critical in capturing the listeners' attention, it is usually best to skip perfunctory remarks about the weather and such. Rather, begin with a real interest grabber—an opening that will pique curiosity about the rest of the message and gain the listener's immediate attention.

There are a number of fascinating approaches to jump starting your listeners into thinking, "Wow! This is going to be an engrossing message."

1. The Startling Statement

Make your first words stunning, surprising, alarming so that your listeners will wonder what on earth you are talking about and where you are going to go with the rest of your message. For example, a sermon on "Raising Righteous Children in an Unrighteous World" might begin like this.

> Last night there were three rapes, five muggings, and seven murders in my next door neighbor's living room. Shocking? The really shocking thing is that the same thing was happening in homes throughout this nation. No one called the police. In fact, few people thought anything about allowing rapists, terrorists, and murderers to come into their homes, talk with their children, and become their examples.

Certainly we would risk our very lives to keep someone from giving one of our youngsters poison, and yet we have permitted television masquerading as entertainment to poison the minds and sensibilities of our most precious treasure day after day, year after year.

Jesus combined startling words with startling action the day He taught in the synagogue when he called to Him a woman who had been bent over for eighteen years to Him and said, "Woman, you are set free from your ailment." When He laid His hands on her, she immediately stood up straight and began praising God. Of course, this miracle didn't go over too well with the leader of the synagogue who accused Him of breaking the Sabbath. His reply put His opponents to shame, and we are told that "all the multitude rejoiced for all the glorious things that were done by Him" (Luke 13:10-17).

2. The Provocative Question

Ask a rhetorical question or series of questions. Then pause and give the listeners time to reflect on and answer them mentally. Beginning with a provocative question immediately gets your listener involved with you and your message. He or she is immediately challenged, not just to listen, but also to respond mentally to what you are saying. For example, a message about God's having a special purpose in creating each of us might start this way.

Do you ever wonder who you are? To the post office you are "occupant." The bank lists you as 2-1273-04-50. To the telephone company you are (718) 555-5124. Do you ever feel like a prisoner in a world of statistics? A number? A part of a machine? Do you ever feel like saying, "When I die, lay me away gently. Do not fold, bend, spindle, or mutilate me?" I say to you today that you are not just a number or a statistic or an accident. You are the very special creation of the God of the universe, and He had a very special purpose in creating you.

When Jesus began to speak to the crowd about John, He posed several intriguing questions: "What did you go out into the wilderness to see? A reed shaken by the wind? But what then did you go out to see? A man clothed in soft garments?...But what did you go out to see? A prophet?" (Matt. 11:7-9). Jesus used questions with great impact in His ministry. We can, too.

3. Humor that Makes a Point

Few approaches bridge the space between the podium and the pew more quickly and more effectively than carefully crafted humor. Here is an example of an amusing story that could be used effectively in beginning a message on the importance of correctly applying biblical principles:

> Several years ago a doctor taught a Red Cross course in emergency medical assistance to a group of ladies from his church. One evening there was a very serious accident in front of the home of one of the ladies who had taken the class.
>
> At the next session, the lady described the accident. "It was horrible! There was blood everywhere. Gashed heads. Broken bones. Unconscious people. It was a good thing I'm taking this course, or I don't know what I would have done."
>
> Of course, the doctor was pleased. "Then you were able to use what I've taught you?"
>
> "Oh, yes. I put my head between my legs and breathed deeply. I never once felt as though I was going to faint."

4. The Analogy

An analogy can be an effective way of showing how the subject under discussion is like something the listener can easily relate to. Martin Thielen prepared his congregation to observe the Lord's Supper with an analogy from the life of the German theologian Dietrich Bonhoeffer.

> Bonhoeffer had been imprisoned in 1943 for his overt opposition to Adolph Hitler's policies and two years later was executed. In a letter about 10 weeks after his arrest, Bonhoeffer wrote to his parents:
>
> > It is Monday, and I was just sitting down to a dinner of turnips and potatoes when a parcel you sent me by Ruth arrived. Such things give me greater joy than I can say. Although I am utterly convinced that nothing can break the bonds between us, I seem to need some outward token or sign to reassure me. In this way, material things become the vehicles of spiritual realities. I suppose it is rather like the felt need in our religion for sacraments.

After reading the letter, Thielen said: "Bonhoeffer knew his parents loved him. Yet he still hungered for that love to be reaffirmed. He needed to be reminded of their love in a tangible way. His package from home served that purpose, and Bonhoeffer saw the Lord's Supper doing the same."

Thielen ended his sermon by going to the Communion table and saying: "Come, brothers and sisters in Christ, let us partake. A package from home has arrived. Let us eat and drink and be reminded of God's awesome love for his children."[5]

5. The Object

Use your imagination to come up with props that will immediately grab your audience's interest.

A mosaic picture, purchased in Italy, composed of small pieces of marble gets attention for a presentation on God's work in our lives. The author's introduction goes like this.

This is my favorite souvenir from my first trip to Europe. Several members from our tour group visited a mosaic studio in Florence, Italy. We watched in fascination as the artist tediously filed away at the tiny pieces of marble with his miniature tools. We were in awe of his patience and skill in making the small bits interlock smoothly. Time and time again, he would try the pieces and then continue the smoothing process until they fit perfectly into the marble mosaic picture his hands were creating.

Finally, after much concentrated effort, he was satisfied with the result. He then turned the picture face down and applied two different types of hot resin or glue to set the pieces firmly in place. The back of the picture was ugly...a huge mess.

Ah, but after he allowed it to set and turned it over, everyone gasped with delight. They saw an exquisitely beautiful picture made from dozens of small pieces of naturally colored marble.

Nearly everyone who watched the picture take final form wanted to have one of the lovely mosaics to take home. That evening, as I looked at the one I purchased, God showed me that our lives are like this mosaic picture.

God is the artist. Only God knows what the completed picture should look like. Only God has the perfect plan for fitting all the bits and pieces impeccably together.

The filing hurts, and often we don't want to give up things from our lives that hinder our spiritual development and relationship with God. And we definitely don't like that hot glue that keeps us still enough to hear God's voice and to stick to God's plan.

Often we don't understand what's happening or why God permits a certain experience or problem in our lives. That's because we're looking at the back side, or we're up too close to see the total picture.

But the exciting thing is that, if we give God free rein, the Master Artist will create a magnificent masterpiece out of our lives.

My souvenir hangs on the dining room wall by the entrance to the kitchen. Three times a day this beautiful mosaic reminds me to trust the Master Artist with the work He is doing each moment in my life.

6. The Anecdote

Jesus recognized that people are always interested in an intriguing, well-told story. Examples of His use of dramatic tales include the stories of the sower and the seed, the foolish virgins, the lost sheep, and many more.

William J. Bausch wrote,

"Stories are appealing because narrative is written into our nature. We are a narrative people. They are appealing because we have an innate curiosity. We want to hear the ending. We want to know "whodunit." They are appealing because they have many layers of meaning and so they "rinse" through us long after we hear them. Think of a good movie that sticks with you for many days, perhaps years. That's testimony to the ruminating power of story."[6]

The following true story would set the scene nicely for a message about Christ's sacrifice on the cross being for you personally.

Amy woke up earlier than usual. After all, the three-year-old was going to her very first circus! Her father James had never seen her as excited.

Her eyes sparkled as they drove across town to the circus grounds. Once there, he had to hold her hand tightly to keep her from running ahead of him. Finally they found their seats in the stands. "When's it going to start, Daddy? When's it going to start?" He pointed out the three rings and showed her where to look for the beginning of the big parade.

Finally, the fanfare of trumpets sounded. Amy's eyes were wide with amazement as she watched the colorful procession. She clapped her hands to the music and squealed with delight as she watched the dancing bears. Her eyes darted back and forth, not knowing which of the three rings to watch.

Suddenly she became very still and quiet. James looked over at her to make sure she was all right. "What is it, Amy?"

"Oh, Daddy." Her voice—indeed her whole being—was filled with awe. "Daddy, they did all this just for me."

We also stand in awe as our thoughts go back to quite a different scene. Three stark crosses on a hill called Golgotha. No brass bands. No tumbling clowns. Only agony and death. We see the lifeless form on that cross in the middle. One who chose to be there, to take our place and give us the amazing gift of eternal life with him. And we say in wonder, "He did it just for me."

7. The News Story

Excellent material can be found by being on the lookout in the newspaper or on the evening news for stories about real people. This real story about Mabel Schoonover is analogous to the attitude of many about the effectiveness of the church in today's society.

Over the past several decades, the church has gradually lost its exalted position of universal respect and reverence in contemporary society. In fact, sometimes the church's current status reminds me of Mabel Schoonover of Floral City, Florida.

It seems that seventy-year-old Mabel Schoonover was declared dead, bureaucratically, by Medicare. It all started when she got a letter addressed to "The Estate of M. Schoonover." This is how she described her experience.

"They told me in Jacksonville that it was a mistake. I told them I knew that already and they said it was the computer. I told the social security office that those idiots in Jacksonville have me dead. They assured me it would take 60 days before they could get me alive and I said it didn't take 60 days to get me dead."

Finally, the bureaucracy returned her from limbo to full life in early September.

Well, the reason that Mabel Schoonover makes me think of the status of the church today is this: I think we've already been declared dead—or at least dying—by a lot of people. In fact, I think some of the prophets of doom have already held the funeral and are just waiting for the lid to be closed on the casket.

Now Mabel may have varicose veins, high blood pressure, and a touch of arthritis, but she's a long way from kicking the bucket. And so is the church.

8. The Hypothetical Story

Take the facts and statistics and make up a story about a particular, but imaginary, person who exemplifies your point. In other words, put flesh and feet on your facts. Use your imagination to turn statistics into believable-sounding people. For example, after saying that one in five children lives in a home where the mother is head of the family, talk about a particular family in that situation. Give them names and make them come to life rather than just reciting, for example, how much less money the average woman makes than the average man. This approach will keep your audience's interest, and they'll remember little Suzi a lot longer than a bald statistic.

The following story was the opening of a presentation about the church's responsibility to minister to and meet the needs of the community, addressing the growing phenomenon of latch-key children:

Cindy Cassidy is a six-year-old first-grader at O. M. Roberts Elementary School in Dallas. An attractive child...somewhat shy and small for her age. She arrives at her apartment at 2:30 p.m., looks furtively all around, in every direction. She then takes the key from her tiny purse, unlocks the door, and goes inside.

First, she makes sure the door is securely locked and checks out the layout of the small apartment. Then she calls her mother at work and reports that she's arrived home safely before settling down to watch TV at a low volume.

There's a knock on the door. She sits motionless...scarcely daring to breathe until she hears the footsteps fade away into the distance.

The phone rings. "My Mommy's in the shower and can't come to the phone right now," she tries to say convincingly.

Cindy is a virtual prisoner for two hours every afternoon until her older brother gets home from high school around 4:30. Her mother arrives about 6:00.

It's not that Cindy's mother wants it that way...not at all. She worries about the tiny girl...especially in the area where they live...not exactly the best neighborhood. But she had been happy to finally find a place where she could pay the rent on her limited income. As to day-care after school...that's a luxury the divorcee simply can't afford.

Cindy is one of a growing number of hundreds of thousands of latch-key children living in a single-parent family at the borderline poverty level in communities throughout the nation. These are tots taught by their parents to fear for their very lives because—all too often—that's exactly what's at stake.

9. Reference to a Movie, Television Program, or Play

Set the scene by using a quote or sequence from a familiar movie, television show, or play. For example, an episode of *Candid Camera* provided an analogy for a message on the stabilizing force of faith in a frenzied world:

A drop-dead gorgeous woman stood inside the lobby of a luxurious office building with a huge suitcase by her side. She would wait for a young, muscular man to come in. Then she would ask if he could possibly help her get the suitcase to her office. "It's just too heavy for me," she would say helplessly as she batted her eyelashes at the unsuspecting guy. Of course, each one was eager to carry her suitcase. He would pick it up and off they would start down the corridor making small talk. Things would go well—until they got to her office. She would open the door, go in and say, "Thank you so very much. You can just put it over here." The man would start to turn the corner, but, to his amazement, he had a very difficult time pointing the suitcase in the right direction. He would try and try, but the suitcase strongly resisted turning from its set course.

Embarrassed, he would make several valiant tries to get the suitcase inside before she finally revealed the problem. He was on *Candid Camera*, and a gyroscope set to go straight ahead had been placed inside the suitcase.

Faith can be the gyroscope that sets one's life toward God's goals and operating procedures for life. Regardless of the direction others are taking or the craziness that may be happening around us, once a person becomes faith-filled, that faith can become the gyroscope that sets the direction for a person's life and keeps that person centered on God's course.

10. A Children's Story or Rhyme

There is a lot of good material in children's stories. Have you read *Winnie the Pooh* or *The Emperor's New Clothes* lately? If not, get out your old storybooks or visit the library to discover just how much depth and philosophy so-called children's stories contain.

For example, the story of Alice in *Through the Looking Glass* can be used to illustrate the difference between viewing our circumstances as they appear naturally or viewing them through the lenses of faith.

Is there anyone here today who doesn't have a single problem? Don't be shy. Just raise your hand. Or better yet, stand up. The rest of us would like to rejoice with you. (Pause.) You mean no one fits into that category? The real surprise would be if anyone did. We all have problems—some of them so severe that it's going to take at least a minor miracle to solve them.

Today I want to point you in the direction of solving them, not by quoting Scripture but by relating the advice of a rather bizarre character. You remember the story, I'm sure—Alice in Lewis Carroll's *Through the Looking Glass*, with its wild and wonderful assortment of characters—the Cheshire Cat, the Mad Hatter, and the White Rabbit, to name a few. In the story, Alice got into a big confrontation with the Queen of Hearts at the Queen's croquet party. Between yelling "Off with their heads," the Queen had made what Alice considered a really absurd statement. Alice's response to the Queen? "One can't believe impossible things."

The Queen shot back, "I daresay you haven't had much practice. When I was your age, I always did it for half an hour a day. Why, sometimes I've believed as many as six impossible things before breakfast."

Now that was good advice. We need to practice believing impossible things. Or, to put it another way, to begin believing the God of the possible when we're faced with a situation so devastating, so overwhelming, that we want to throw up our hands and label it as an "impossible thing."

Before breakfast is a good time to start practicing believing the God of the possible can and will turn the impossible into, not only the possible, but the "done deal."

The God who parted the Red Sea to save the Israelites....The God who gave Sarah and Abraham a son in their old age....The God who gave Elijah victory over the priests of Baal by sending fire to consume the altar....The God who turned around (pause)…just fill in the blank with your impossible thing. And then start believing that God can and will turn your impossible thing into the possible.

11. Quote a Famous Person, an Authority, or the Results of a Study

Quoting an expert or the conclusion of a study on your subject lends weight to your words.

One speech, "Women as Leaders? What Was Jesus' View?" begins with the results of a study.

Want to be the chief executive officer of a great American corporation? Be born in the Middle West. Go to college in the East and be—if at all possible—a man.

That's the message of a study on chief executives, conducted by the executive-recruiting firm of Arthur Young Executive Resource Consultants, involving eight hundred business leaders. One person associated with the study concluded flatly that the odds favor a woman's being elected President of the United States over a woman's becoming a chief executive officer of any of the top five hundred U.S. industrial companies. The population inside the executive ranks is estimated at less than one percent female. At this time, there just aren't many women cast in that role.

In other words, things haven't changed too much since Shakespeare's days. He didn't write many good parts for women either. And most of the women he did include didn't turn out too well. Lady Macbeth was a murderer. Desdemona was killed by her jealous husband, and Ophelia committed suicide.

One of Shakespeare's heroines did fare somewhat better. Portia in The Merchant of Venice saved the merchant's life with her clever arguments. But, of course, to be acceptable to the audiences of Shakespeare's time, Portia had to be disguised as a man. The result is an interesting paradox — reluctant acceptance and, on the other hand, known ability.

Of course, I don't have to tell you that that analogy extends from the boundaries of the stage to the real life status that society has accorded females for a long, long time.

Things were really gloomy for the female sex in Jesus' day. The remarkable respect He accorded women and the affirmation He gave them by his words and actions was unheard of. For example, when He called the woman in the temple "a daughter of Abraham," everyone, including the women who were present, must have been shocked. Men had been referred to as sons of Abraham, but a woman as a daughter of Abraham? Unheard of. And when He, a rabbi, actually taught women, He must have raised a lot of eyebrows. Even more jolting was the fact that women followed after Him and (as evidenced by the usage of the language) did the same types of things as the disciples.

12. The Gimmick

Think of some cute or folksy approach to get your audience's attention. For example, a speech on Christian leadership could be built around the three Zs with each point being built on a word starting with a Z.

> *My first Z is zoom.*
> *My next Z is zeal.*
> *My last Z is zest.*

13. The Theme Approach

An interesting way to provide continuity and help keep the listener's mind "on track" is to use a central theme or thread throughout the presentation. This can be done by weaving a story in and out of the message, using an appropriate proverb to make each point, or telling anecdotes about a certain animal or historical happening.

The theme of *The Wizard of Oz* became the structure for a baccalaureate message to high school students:

Today we're going to be talking about a story you probably read when you were in grade school. Or perhaps you saw the movie — *The Wizard of Oz*. What an intriguing plot — lots of suspense, action, and colorful characters. It's also an allegory packed with nuggets of truth and wisdom for successful living.

You will recall that each of the principal characters — Dorothy, the Scarecrow, the Tin Woodman, and the Cowardly Lion — was searching for something. The Scarecrow for a brain; the Woodman, a heart; and the Lion, courage. They were told that the Wizard could give them their heart's desire, so they set off to follow the yellow brick road to take them to the land of Oz.

Dorothy wanted to go back to Kansas, where everything would be just as it had always been. And she was counting on the yellow brick road to take her there. What Dorothy didn't realize — and we can learn from her — is that we can never go back. The one never-changing certainty of life is that nothing ever stays the same — that everything changes — people, our relationships, circumstances. Nothing will ever be again quite the same as it is this evening.

...I hope you have learned to savor each moment as you go—because your yellow brick road is a one-way street, and you can only move forward. Or, as Thomas Wolfe said, "You can't go home again."

As for Dorothy's traveling companions—the Lion, the Tin Woodman, and the Scarecrow—each of them was expecting the Wizard to solve all of their problems. Certainly others can provide guideposts along the way.

...What the Lion, the Tin Woodman, and the Scarecrow learned on their trip is a lesson for us all. They found out that the Wizard of Oz couldn't give them their heart's desire. In fact, they learned he was just a phony without any power to help them at all. What they did discover was that the solution to their problem had to come from within themselves, that they had to make their own pathway on a journey no one else could take for them. They also discovered that they had already been given all the personal resources they needed for making their dreams come true.

...The last thing I think we can learn from the Wizard of Oz is that adversity and obstacles are often very important stepping stones on our journey. The Wicked Witch of the West and the Wizard himself endangered the security of the yellow-brick-road travelers. Yet it was through those difficult experiences that they discovered their own inner strength and potential.

As graduates, it's wonderful to know that you have family, friends, and faculty cheering you on and rooting for you both now and in the years to come. But remember! You have to make the journey yourself. With God's help, you can discover and successfully travel your yellow brick road.

The Statement of Purpose

After you get the audience's attention and have them hooked with a good, strong opening, it's time to state the purpose of your message. What are you going to tell them? What are they going to get out of listening to what you have to say? The statement of purpose should be stated succinctly and crisply in two or three sentences.

Here is an example of a statement of purpose:

> Today we will be talking about the advantages of having family devotions in the home. I'll be giving you some workable suggestions for involving every member of the family. And I hope that, if you're not already taking advantage of this wonderful approach to building strong family ties, you'll be ready to make family devotions a part of your daily routine.

The Body of the Speech

The body of the speech, of course, is the meat of the message. Although there are many possible formats, one that works well is the message with three points. For some reason, people seem to like to think in groups of three. The audience will usually remember three things at a time. It is especially effective to use your fingers as a visual gesture as you discuss each point. Numbering the points helps, too. Make statements like these: "The first thing I would like to say about…" "My second point is…" The third thing you need to know about…."

For example, when using the "gimmick approach" as an introduction technique, as previously mentioned, you would want to elaborate on each one of the three Zs.

1. First of all, as a leader you need to zoom out ahead of obstacles and zoom in on your major goals and responsibilities. This means leading by example rather than by clout.

2. Second, use zeal in your dedication and enthusiasm for creating an atmosphere for open communication. You can find specific ways to create this atmosphere, in various settings, with examples from outstanding Christian leaders.

3. Third, the zest for your leadership position is necessary to build a spirit of unity, a oneness of purpose. That unity has to start at the top with whose who lead.

Use case histories and real-life examples of zest and the positive results of leading with zest.

There is also something about listing that seems to motivate people to take notes on what you are saying. Start telling your audience that you are going to give them ten ways to overcome a problem, and watch the pencils and paper come out.

Keep your points simple, couched in everyday terminology. Of course, coming up with the three main points can be a challenge. Initially you may want to write down the following about the topic:

I believe....

I think....

I feel....

Ask yourself, "What are the major units or thought concepts I want to communicate?" After that, come up with the supporting evidence: Scripture, statistics, quotations (but make sure they're from people known to the listeners, and people who matter to them), stories, facts, illustrations—things that will add life to each unit. Also, consider which audiovisual aids would enhance and add interest to your presentation.

Check your transitions. Be sure you are not going abruptly from one thought to something completely different. You don't want to leave your listener back at the last thought station while you continue on at one hundred miles an hour. Remember that listeners cannot go back and reread what you have just said. You have to take them slowly and smoothly to your next point.

The Conclusion

The conclusion of the speech needs to be strong and delivered with punch. After all, this is your last shot at them.

State in the final moments what you want your listeners to take away with them. Review what you have said. Summarize the main points to remind them once more of what you've covered.

Give the listeners a challenge, a plan of action. Give them specific steps they can take to make what you've described a reality.

Then to wrap it all up in a neat package, tie the end back to your introduction.

To put it simply:

Tell them what you're going to tell them.

Tell them.

Tell them what you told them.

Make It Personal

Consider: Repetition of fact can be deadly dull for an audience. People are more interested in hearing about people—those they can relate to—than things.

Statistics can be impressive—up to a point. A recital of numbers can soon result in nodding heads and snoring listeners. Use your imagination to turn your statistics into flesh-and-bone people. Find out about a particular person included in your statistics by calling a social service agency for an anonymous description. Or make up a person or family that could realistically fit into such a situation. This approach will keep your audience's interest, and they'll remember a person you've made real to them a lot longer than a bald statistic.

Use personal examples when appropriate. Examples from your own life help your audience relate to you as a human being and make you seem more like an old friend. It's amazing how many really good illustrations for speeches occur in our day-to-day lives—once we start looking for them. Keep a small notebook handy to jot down situations as they occur or as you remember them.

Use names of people in the audience in telling a hypothetical (or real) story. However, be sure they will enjoy the attention, or ask their permission. If you don't know anyone in the group, you will have to rely on the program chairman or others to give you the name of someone who will like being talked about. Using names is an excellent rapport builder.

Relate a point to the specific needs and interests of your audience. You may refer to their particular occupation (or types of work), their age groups, or their community. Or relate a point or story to a specific individual in the audience. You could say, for example, "I'm sure Johnny Martin could tell us a lot about body language from his experience as a salesman."

Arrive early enough to get acquainted with some members of the audience, and say something like: "I was talking with Kathy Holland before dinner, and she said...."

Refer to something the group experienced together, e.g., something another speaker said.

SPEECH ORGANIZATION FORM

Title _____

_____

What is the purpose of my speech? _____

_____

_____

How will I open the speech to get my audience's attention? _____

_____

_____

What is my statement of purpose? _____

_____

_____

What main points do I want to make? _____

_____

_____

What examples, anecdotes, humor, statistics, quotations, etc. can I use to support my main points? _____

_____

_____

What audiovisual approaches would enhance my presentation?

_____

_____

How can I briefly summarize what I have said to make my audience remember my main points? _____

_____

_____

How will I close my speech to make it memorable? _____

_____

_____

Chapter 8

GETTING READY FOR THE BIG EVENT

*And in a window sat a certain young man named Eutychus,
who was sinking into a deep sleep. He was overcome by
sleep; and as Paul continued speaking, he fell down from the
third story and was taken up dead (Acts 20:9).*

How Long Is Long Enough?

Consider: The Lord's Prayer, the Twenty-third Psalm, and Lincoln's Gettysburg Address are considered three of the great literary treasures of all time. Not one of them is more than three hundred words in length.

Brevity in speaking is an asset that people appreciate. Someone has said: "He that thinketh by the inch and talketh by the yard should be kicked by the foot."[1] As a speaker, you don't want your audience to feel as though you're holding them hostage while you drone on and on. Unless you have a proven track record of raising people from the dead, as Paul did in the case of Eutychus, you would do well to match the length of your presentation to the interest span of your listeners.

Speaking past that interest point of the listener is kind of like adding water to milk. You'll end up with more liquid, but the quality and taste will suffer. Speaking too long can water down the effectiveness of your message.

It is important to find out from the program chairperson exactly how long he or she wants you to speak. Then observe that time limit religiously. It is considered extremely rude to go over the allotted time, since most meetings and programs are carefully planned for a certain time frame. Also, you are unfair to those who will be appearing on the program later if you wear the audience down to a nub.

Even if you have not been given a time limit, consider the ability of your audience to sit still and concentrate. There is real truth in the saying "The mind can comprehend only what the seat can endure." In all probability, your presentation will last longer when you actually give it than it did in rehearsal. A good rule of thumb to follow is to allow a little more time for the presentation than it takes to rehearse, in order to allow time for audience response and those few extra remarks you may decide spontaneously to throw in.

An old country preacher used to start his sermons with this prayer:

> *Lord, fill my mouth*
> *With worthwhile stuff,*
> *And nudge me when*
> *I've said enough.*

Or, in the words of an old farmer, "When you're through pumping, let go the handle."[2]

Preparation and Use of Notes

Consider: People come to hear a speaker speak, not read. Very few people can read from a script and maintain the audience's interest and attention.

As a rule, a speaker will do a much better job using brief notes written or typed on a few index cards. Of course, approaches vary with the individual, and you really have to find out what works best for you.

For some speakers a full-blown script serves as a security blanket—in case their minds go blank and they completely forget what to say. Usually they do not plan to use the script in its entirety, only to have it handy just in case. However, often speakers will end up reading a lot more than they had intended to—especially if they become nervous.

Other speakers try to memorize the entire speech—word for word. This approach can be very dangerous—particularly if there are major distractions during the speech, such as a waiter who drops a tray of dishes or a crying baby.

One of the best approaches, one that will work well for most speakers, is this: memorize the opening of your speech and go over it several times. The first few moments are important for developing rapport, and you should be free to look at the audience without interruption.

List your major points and key phrases (to remind you, for example, of an anecdote you plan to use) on 8 1/2 x 5 1/2 inch index cards. Use a symbol or a color to indicate the use of audiovisual material. For example, a large T in a box, followed by #1, #2, etc., could indicate where you will use a transparency. Include direct quotations and statistics that you will want to read.

Number your points. Doing so will help you keep track of where you are.

Use indentation, color coding, or what-have-you to help keep you on track and to remind you to emphasize a point. Develop your own system—what will work best for you—and stick with it.

Memorize the very end of your speech so that you can conclude with a powerful close, looking directly at your audience.

Of course, there may be an occasion when you will almost have to use a formal word-for-word script. You may need a script, for example, in making a major policy statement address, or if the material is of an extremely sensitive nature or has legal ramifications. If you do need a script, it is critically important to go over and over and over it, reading aloud. Try a color highlighter for words or phrases you want to emphasize.

Here are some things to remember in preparing your notes.

- Make sure the writing or type is large enough to see when you are standing at the speaker's stand—even if the light isn't as good as you would like it to be.

- Use as few cards or pages as possible. The less you have to manipulate, the better off you are.

- Number your cards—just in case you drop them or they get mixed up.

- Use only one side of the cards so you don't have to turn them over. Otherwise, under the pressure of the moment, you may turn the card over...and then back over again.

- Don't fold your speech if you have it on paper. Chances are it will never be the same again as far as resting flatly on the lectern out of view of the audience.

- Don't use a ring binder or a pad. Flipping pages are distracting to the audience.
- Slide cards or pages over as you finish using them rather than stacking them under the unused pages.
- Be sure your stack of cards or pages can rest safely on the speaker's stand without sliding off if it's made at an angle.
- Hang onto your notes as if they were made of gold. Putting them down and expecting them to stay there can be hazardous to your speaking health.

Rehearsing

Consider: Epictetus, the Stoic philosopher, once said, "No great thing is created suddenly, any more than a bunch of grapes or a fig. If you tell me that you desire a fig, I answer you that there must be time. Let it first blossom, then bear fruit, then ripen."[3]

All of us have seen a seasoned, polished speaker and thought how easy it looks. But one thing's for sure: if it looks easy, a lot of hard, tedious work has gone into that presentation before the speaker steps up on the podium.

Careful preparation is one of the greatest boons to self-confidence a speaker can have. Lawrence M. Briggs said, "You can't usually tell whether a man is a finished speaker until he sits down."[4] But if when you sit down you want people to think you're a finished speaker, not just finished speaking, you'll have to pay the price of thorough rehearsal.

Sir Winston Churchill, who moved and inspired men and women around the world with his words, understood the vital necessity of being well prepared and practicing his speeches. Somehow he always managed to find time to rehearse down to the finest detail.

A wonderful story is told about the way Churchill took advantage of every opportunity to practice. It seems that on one occasion, his valet thought he heard Churchill say something through the bathroom door as he was taking a bath. His valet tapped on the door and said, "Excuse me, sir, but were you speaking to me?" "No," Churchill replied, "I was addressing the House of Commons."[5]

The old saying "practice makes perfect" may be trite, but it's true.

Going through your entire presentation four to six times is a good way to ensure thorough familiarity and confidence in being able to deliver your material smoothly. There are several ways to rehearse. Ideally, try to simulate as much as possible the actual conditions you will be facing.

After going through the presentation two or three times, use some method of getting feedback. Videotaping yourself gives the advantage of being able to see yourself as others see you. It is ideal for honing gestures, facial expressions, enunciation, and other mechanics of speaking. Try to get a friend or member of your family to serve as an audience and give you feedback on clarity, interest maintenance, length, vocabulary, and all those other things that make or break a speaker. In case you don't have access to videotaping equipment and can't con anyone into listening to your rehearsal, practice in front of a mirror to see how you look, and audio tape your voice.

Practice with an object the right height for a speaker's stand. Part of your rehearsal should be manipulating your note cards. One very important thing is this: if you will be using audiovisual equipment, be sure to practice handling transparencies or changing the pages on a flip chart. Otherwise, it's very easy to get bogged down in the mechanics of operating the equipment and forget or foul up what you're saying.

Above all in rehearsing, be aware of the need to sound excited, enthusiastic, and confident of what you're saying.

Winston Churchill believed that the style of the orator is not nearly as important as his sincerity. "Before he can inspire them with any emotion, he must be swayed by it himself. When he would rouse their indignation, he must be swayed by it himself. Before he can move their tears, his own must flow. To convince them he must himself believe. His opinions may change as their impressions fade, but every orator means what he says at the moment he says it. He may be often inconsistent. He is never consciously insincere."[6]

Or, in a lighter vein, every speaker would do well to follow this advice of a veteran circus star to a would-be flying trapeze performer: "Throw your heart over the bars and your body will follow."[7]

Writing Your Own Introduction

A very important aspect of preparing to give a speech is to write your own introduction. After all, the way you are introduced to your audience will be critical to your initial acceptance by that audience.

Unfortunately, many introducers do the speaker a gross injustice by making him or her sound deadly dull or by trying to steal the spotlight from the speaker. When this happens, the speaker has a real challenge. It may take the first three or four minutes to overcome the damage the introducer has done to you as the speaker.

As a speaker, you are taking a major risk when you send an introducer your vita. Have you ever gotten really excited about hearing a speaker once you have sat through a lackluster recital of his birth, every place he went to school, names and ages of children, every position he has held, and on and on ad nauseam? If you are a person of many accomplishments, this reading will probably cut into the time allotted for your remarks besides getting your audience so bored they'll be ready to bolt out the door.

Since this is the case, you might want to seriously consider writing your own introduction and making sure that the person who is going to introduce you receives it. Most people who have been given the thankless task of introducing you will be relieved that they don't have to bother with trying to make up their own introduction. In case, though, that you're concerned that they might be offended, you might title it "background information" rather than "introduction."

Even if you've sent the introducer your introduction in the mail, it's a good idea to take a copy with you to the occasion…just in case the original was lost or forgotten. Then check with the person to be sure he or she has it.

Writing your own introduction gives you the opportunity to include only the information about yourself that you believe will be of particular interest to your audience. You also can include past experience and qualifications that lend credibility to your speaking on that specific subject. You can decide whether you want the title of your speech given in the introduction. You may have reason to reveal your title yourself, particularly if you plan to use provocative questions to make your audience really wonder what you're leading up to. Another advantage of writing your own introduction is that your opening remarks will, seemingly spontaneously, tie into the introduction.

Having your own introduction ready may save you from the embarrassment of the introducer's giving erroneous information, telling weird stories, or turning off your audience before you even have a chance to walk to the speaker's stand.

Many details are important in getting ready for the big event. And they're all worth the time and effort of a successful and impactful presentation.

Jenkin Lloyd Jones said, "A speech is a solemn responsibility. The man who makes a bad 30-minute speech to 200 people wastes only a half hour of his own time. But he wastes 100 hours of the audience's time—more than four days—which should be a hanging offense."[8]

Chapter 9

SIXTEEN TYPES OF SPEECHES

*Praying always with all prayer and supplication in the
Spirit, being watchful to this end with all perseverance and
supplication for all the saints—and for me, that utterance
may be given to me, that I may open my mouth boldly to
make known the mystery of the gospel, for which I am an
ambassador in chains; that in it I may speak boldly, as I
ought to speak (Eph. 6:18-20).*

Consider: Speaking engagements, like notes at the bank, finally
come due. It would be impossible even to list all the different
types of occasions and situations a speaker might encounter.
However, there are certain kinds of speeches that a speaker is more
likely to be asked to give.

The guidelines and samples of some genres of speeches in this
chapter should prove helpful to the person who, out of the blue, is
asked to make a certain kind of speech.

Responsibilities of the Master of Ceremonies

Consider: The master of ceremonies is like the minor official at
a bullfight whose main function is to open and close the gates to let
the bull in and out.[1]

Serving as master of ceremonies is a very important role. In fact
the success (or failure) of the whole meeting or event will depend on
how well you do your job.

The master of ceremonies sets the tone for the whole meeting. It's
difficult for a speaker to overcome a boring emcee or one who sets an
inappropriate tone for the occasion. However, a good emcee will have
the audience eager to hear what other speakers have to say.

Here are some important things to keep in mind.

- An emcee needs to be not only a good speaker but also attentive to detail. It is important for the emcee to arrive early to check out all the arrangements for the meeting and to correct any problems — before the meeting begins.
- The emcee must keep the meeting moving and on schedule. A too-long meeting can turn into a tragedy — especially for a banquet speaker who is introduced at 10:30 p.m. to give the main address.
- The emcee should make sure that the room temperature remains comfortable and have it adjusted if it gets too hot or too cold.
- The emcee must be prepared for emergencies.
- The emcee should make the people she or he introduces sound interesting and exciting to the audience.
- The emcee should not try to be the main attraction, the star of the show. Rather, the emcee's role is to act as a facilitator to keep things on track and running smoothly.

A person who is called on to act as emcee would do well to know the protocol for seating at a formal banquet. Here's the way it goes.

If space permits at the head table, spouses of program participants may also be seated there. But be sure either to seat none of the spouses at the head table or all of them. An exception might be the spouse of a person being honored if there is not room for the others.

The host or person presiding should be seated at the center of the head table.

To the right of center should be the person being honored, or, if there's not an honoree, the main speaker. In case there is an honoree, the featured speaker should be seated to the host's or presider's left with an emcee seated by the main speaker.

Other head-table guests should be seated alternately right, left, right, left, according to their rank or importance.

If possible, program participants should be seated at the head table to prevent unnecessarily long pauses in the program while members of the audience come to the podium.

CHECKLIST FOR THE MASTER OF CEREMONIES

❑ Is the mike (if one is to be used) turned on, working properly, and set at the appropriate sound level?

❑ Does the speaker's stand have a light that works, or is it located in a well-lighted area?

❑ Is the room a little too cool for comfort? It will warm up as people start arriving.

❑ Do you know where the thermostat is located and how to adjust the room temperature?

❑ Have you checked the location of wall plugs, if audiovisual equipment is to be used? Are extension cords available, if needed? Are extension cords taped down to the floor to prevent tripping? Are appropriate stands available? Is equipment in place and operating correctly? Is a screen located for optimum viewing by the audience? Do you have extra projector bulbs ready in case one burns out? Have you made arrangements for someone to turn the lights off and on, on cue, if this is needed?

❑ Is the room arranged in the best possible way for this particular occasion?

❑ In the case of a dinner meeting, have you made arrangements for tables not to be cleared while the speaker is presenting? Table-clearing can be extremely distracting—really death for the success of a speech.

❑ Do you have the information needed to make interesting introductions?

❑ Do you have in mind some filler material you can use in case there is an unavoidable delay?

❑ If there is to be a head table, do you have the names and titles of those who should be introduced?

The program for a banquet would go something like this.

1. Emcee or person presiding (e.g., club president) makes very brief welcoming remarks including a reference to the occasion.

2. Emcee introduces person giving invocation.

3. Invocation is given.

4. Emcee leads or introduces person to lead the Pledge of Allegiance and national anthem (if used).

5. Dinner begins, with head table being served first.

6. Emcee thanks the musicians (if there is dinner music) and introduces those seated at the head table (leading in applause after each introduction, or asking guests to please hold their applause until everyone has been introduced).

7. Emcee introduces main speaker or introduces person to make introduction.

8. Speaker delivers remarks.

9. Emcee continues applause and thanks speaker, other participants, planners of the occasion, and guests, and calls for the benediction.

10. Benediction.

Speech of Introduction

Usually a major task of the emcee will be the introduction of the main speaker, although sometimes someone else will be asked to do the honor. The speech of introduction is very important to the audience and to the speaker. It should knit the two together for the time they will spend with one another.

Here are five steps to an effective introduction.

1. Give a preview of the speaker, his or her affiliation, and the topic (unless the speaker has requested that you not reveal this information).

2. Present the speaker's credentials. Why is this particular speaker uniquely qualified to speak on this particular topic?

3. Identify the importance of the subject.

4. Show how the speech will benefit this particular audience.

5. Set an appropriate level for anticipation and excitement at the conclusion of the introduction by vocal enthusiasm and leading the audience in applause.

These are some important points to keep in mind when you're called on to introduce someone.

- The speech of introduction should be brief, not over two or three minutes.

- Your role as an introducer is to get the audience ready to listen to the main speaker—not to call attention to yourself.

- You should tell enough about the person to get the audience interested and to give him or her credibility. However, a long recital of a person's life history is tedious and boring. It can put the audience to sleep rather than get them excited about hearing the speaker. Do give information that will help develop rapport for the speaker. For example, if your speaker is addressing a Kiwanis Club and is a member of another Kiwanis Club, that information would give the audience an immediate common bond with him or her.

- Don't use the occasion to try to be a comedian or to make a speech on the subject yourself. You may steal some of the speaker's material and leave her or him in an awkward position.

- Do find out what the speaker wants you to tell the audience.

- Don't put the speaker on the spot by bragging too much about his or her speaking ability. Don't introduce a speaker as "a silver-tongued orator" or a "speaker without equal." Stick to who the speaker is and what the speaker knows. Let the speaker demonstrate her or his own ability as an orator.

- The introduction should highlight the person's qualifications for speaking on a certain subject, not bury those qualifications in detail. If you are introducing a speaker on a business subject, the fact that the speaker was awarded the Purple Heart while in the service a number of years ago would be relatively unimportant. However, if a veterans' group, they would immediately be interested in hearing what a Purple Heart recipient has to say. The longer a speaker has been

SPEECH OF INTRODUCTION OUTLINE FORM

We are fortunate to have as our speaker today _____,
                                        (full name)
_____.
        (descriptive phrase about position, accomplishment, etc.)
His/her qualifications and experience in this field include _____
_____
_____.

This topic is important because _____
_____.

All of us will benefit from hearing what _____
_____ has to say because _____
_____.

_____ is a native of _____
_____ and a graduate of _____.
Also, _____
        (information about family, awards, hobbies, etc., if pertinent)
_____
_____.

_____'s speech is titled _____
  (speaker's name)
_____.

Please join me in welcoming _____
                                        (speaker's full name)

(Lead applause, shake hands with the speaker when it seems
natural, and be seated.)

out of school the less important it is to tell the audience about degrees. It is better to concentrate on demonstrated performance and recent accomplishments rather than past academic achievements.

- As an introducer, you should project an image of the speaker as a competent, interesting person who is abundantly qualified to speak on the chosen subject.

- Give the title or subject of the speech—unless the speaker asks you not to.

- On occasion you may want to say something to the speaker about the audience in the speech of introduction. For example, you might want to inform the speaker that most of the members had read the speaker's book and requested that he or she be asked to speak.

- The level of dignity or informality of your introduction should depend on the occasion, your relationship with the speaker, and the prestige of the speaker.

- As a rule, the better known the speaker, the shorter the introduction should be. The President of the United States, for example, is always introduced with a statement like this: "Ladies and gentlemen, the President of the United States."

As an introducer, think of yourself holding the speaker by one hand and the audience by your other hand. Then move them together and place each one's hand in the other's. Then move out of the way.

The Persuasive Speech

The basic purposes of the speech of persuasion are to sell an idea to the members of an audience, change their minds about an issue, move them to take a certain action, or accomplish a combination of these purposes.

The basic appeal of the persuasive speech must be made on psychological grounds. It is important, then, to relate what you have to say to the basic drives and motives of the audience. These include physical well-being, acquisition of material well-being, recognition, public approval (desire to be in the "in-crowd"), affection and love of family and friends, and esthetic tastes.

To be an effective persuasive speaker, you must know as much as possible about the makeup and outlook of your audience. These are some considerations to keep in mind.

- What is the average age of the audience? Young people tend to be more liberal and more susceptible to influence, new ideas, and idealistic statements. It takes an energetic, forceful presentation to move them.

- What is the existing belief of the majority of audience members? A more logical approach should be used with a hostile group, while a more psychological approach is more effective with an apathetic audience. Your purpose in addressing apathetic listeners will usually be to move them to take a certain action; with a hostile group, it will be to change opinion.

- What is the background and training of the group? The more highly trained listeners are, the more willing they will be to experiment, to try a different approach or a new idea. The audience with less training will require a more forceful presentation. Those with less education respond positively, in general, to an authoritarian approach. However, a speaker who is cocky or extremely dogmatic will turn any audience off.

- It is very important to make sure the physical needs and comfort of your audience are met if you expect to move them to do something. A too-hot or cold meeting room, a depressing atmosphere, uncomfortable chairs, and long meetings without adequate restroom and refreshment breaks will make your job as a persuader extremely difficult.

- What is the situation of most of your audience members? If half of your listeners are unemployed or work for a business or industry in the process of making cuts, your chances of inspiring them to get behind the arts in their community are practically nil. You have to meet listeners on the level at which they're functioning. The lower, more basic needs (food, shelter, safety) must be met before higher levels can be addressed successfully.

Here are some tips for choosing material to use in a persuasive speech.

- Show your listener what's in it for her or him. Make it personal.
- Choose material that's active.

- Talk about real things—people, locations, dates—rather than the abstract.
- Consider the proximity of the material to the interest and experience of the audience.
- Be sure to use examples, case histories, or anecdotes that are familiar and of value to the group.
- Include material that's novel and unusual.
- Use humor, but sparingly and in good taste.
- Use persuasive words. A study conducted by Yale University researchers showed that the twelve most persuasive words in the English language are these: discovery, easy, guarantee, health, love, money, new, proven, results, safety, save, and you.[2]
- Give your listeners a plan of action if your purpose is to move them to do something. They may feel inspired by your words, but suggesting practical steps they might take may move them from theory toward a constructive goal.
- A question-and-answer session is usually appropriate with the persuasive speech.

The Informative Speech

The purpose of the informative speech is to secure understanding and to assist the listener in learning and evaluating the information presented. The informative approach is appropriately used in teaching, training situations, presentations of reports, demonstrations, and book reviews.

In selecting a topic for the informative speech, keep the following information in mind.

- The nature of the occasion
- Your interest in and convictions about the subject
- Appropriateness to the intellectual background and training of the audience
- Suitability for oral presentation
- Goal for this particular audience in relation to the subject

The following strategies are recommended for gathering material.

- Review of previous knowledge on the subject
- Research in reference books, periodicals, books

- Interviews
- Questionnaires
- Internet

These approaches provide good supportive material for this type of speech.

- Statistical information, rounded off when exactness is not important
- Case histories
- Personal examples
- Audiovisual materials
- Use of charts, graphs, and lists
- Handouts
- Vivid and graphic word pictures
- Definitions
- Statements from authorities
- Comparisons with the familiar, analogies

This type of speech is mostly deductive in form, starting with generalities and moving to specific information. Start with the familiar and move to the unfamiliar, using a sequence of ideas. A chronological approach may also be used effectively. Add a question-and-answer session for maximum benefit for your audience.

The Research Speech

The research speech, while sharing some commonalities with the informative speech, is probably more challenging to present in an effective, engaging way. Of course, we assume that those gathered are interested in hearing the outcomes of your study, or a speech detailing the results of several research projects on a particular subject. This is probably a more serious crowd than most. Nevertheless, the speaker is obligated to make her or his presentation as exciting and pertinent to that particular audience as possible.

These are some good questions about your audience to consider in planning your presentation.

- Is this a group of professionals with a high level of skill and experience related to the research subject?
- Will the audience be a mixture of those who are very knowledgeable on the subject and those who just have an interest?

- Will your listeners be laypersons who, for whatever reason, want to learn more about research findings in the area you will be addressing?

Without specific knowledge about your audience, you probably will be either talking down to the group or speaking way over their heads. For example, a group of senior citizens and a group of physicians might be interested in finding out about the same studies related to aging. But, of course, the manner and detail with which you present the information would be totally different.

While the research presentation is one of the most formal types of speeches, it needn't be dull or without humor. If you are the researcher yourself, chances are some funny or frustrating things happened in the process of conducting your study. If you're speaking to fellow researchers, of course, they will be able to relate to obstacles you had to overcome or puzzling aspects of the process.

A light beginning always helps. For example, if you are asked to speak about the study for your doctoral dissertation, you might say something like this: "I have really been looking forward to talking to you about my study. After all, this may be my only opportunity to tell a group of people who are too polite to get up and leave about all I've done. Even though I find it fascinating, I've noticed that not everyone is interested in hearing all the details." You also might want to make fun of the—no doubt—very long title of your dissertation by saying, "How do you like that for a catchy title?"

Here are some pointers for making the research speech interesting and understandable.

- Tell the audience what is the significance of the research project and its findings to them and to others.
- If you are the researcher, tell your listeners how you became interested in this particular project. That usually makes an intriguing story.
- Use audiovisual approaches that are attention-getting and that promote understanding. For example, instead of merely quoting statistics, you might want to use a colorful pie chart to present the same information in a more graphic way. Or, if you have researched on poverty in an urban area, a color-coded city map could be effective.

- For a lay group, translate statistics into a story about real-sounding but hypothetical people.
- Prepare a handout with facts and statistics. Tell the audience they will receive that information. Otherwise, they may become frustrated in trying to write down a lot of notes unnecessarily.
- Include a question-and-answer session in your allotted time for speaking.

The Entertaining Speech

Although most speakers are not asked very often to give a strictly entertaining speech, there are orators who make a good living specializing in the speech of entertainment. In fact, some of them have just one basic speech they give over and over with only a few changes, such as substituting the names of people in the audience in their stories. Occasionally, however, speakers who don't focus on just this type of speaking are asked to give a speech with the sole purpose of entertaining the audience.

Banquets and class reunions usually draw the majority of requests for this type of speech. Most after-dinner speakers would do well to make at least the first portion of their speeches entertaining, with some humorous oases worked in from time to time. Otherwise, they may find themselves speaking to after-dinner nappers.

The use of humor in any speech has many advantages.

1. Humor gets attention.

2. Humor creates a sense of togetherness within the audience. It becomes a community activity, bonding the participants. Even strangers will smile at one another and nod in agreement as they share the delightfully pleasant experience of laughing together.

3. Humor creates rapport between the audience and the speaker.

4. Humor provides an instant and simple way for an audience to participate in the presentation. No longer are they just sitting there with folded hands. They are doing something. And it's fun!

5. Humor can provide a release for tension. A very heavy topic or a session where emotions are running high can

use the leaven of at least a few smiles or chuckles. A dose of humor can make a controversial or hard message more palatable to the listener.

6. Humor can transform a mistake from a potentially awkward and embarrassing situation, for the speaker and the audience, into a special moment of enjoyment for all.

7. The speaker who is the brunt of his or her true funny story can make a special connection with an audience. Self-disclosive humor can be used effectively to say, "Hey, I'm one of you. These things happen to me, too." This kind of humor dispels the impression that the speaker is trying to appear to be perfect and is talking down to the audience.

8. Using humor effectively in church negates the misconception that being a Christian is boring and takes the fun out of life.

9. Humor can be used effectively to prepare the listener to receive your message. When people laugh, they drop their defenses and become more open to receiving the gospel.

10. Humor enlarges our perspective. It gives new lenses through which we see a multi-faceted view. David Rees commented: "Humor helps us step back and see things in a different way. It gives us a fresh eye, allowing us to see things sideways, backward, upside down, and inside out."[3]

When you're giving a strictly entertaining speech, you should consider three main things: the makeup of the audience, the occasion, and yourself as a speaker.

Getting people to laugh is great. But what if you've never been able to tell a joke? Some people are born with a great sense of timing, but then some of us aren't. What then?

Even if you feel comically deprived, you can still get a mirthful response with an amusing story. You don't have to use a joke to get a laugh. Anyone can be funny within the parameters of his or her comfort zone. Humor does not have to result in people doubled over in laughter to be effective.

Here are some approaches that are effective in developing a humorous speech.

- Use a theme for your humorous speech rather than presenting a series of unrelated jokes or stories. Be sure to use transitions to tie anecdotes together.
- The entertaining speech should be as carefully prepared and rehearsed as any other speech, perhaps more so.
- Learn your stories so well that you don't have to refer to notes. Reading a joke will rarely result in a laugh.
- The style of delivery should be intimate—as though you're merely talking with the audience.
- Make yourself the humorous object of the stories.
- Direct humor to the group or to someone in the audience. However, using humor that is directed at a person or group must be carefully evaluated. It is all right to use stories that laugh with a group, especially if you are a member of that group, but it is highly questionable to laugh at a group.
- Tell stories on well-known members of the audience. However, be sure you either know them well enough to be certain they will enjoy the attention or have their permission in advance.
- Pick up on current events. You can build humor around a particular activity in your church or group, a popular movie, and what you hear people talking about.
- Localize your humor. If the joke takes place in a hotel lobby, place it in the hotel where you are speaking at a banquet, or in one that is well-known—a place your listeners can visualize and identify with.
- Be sure to speak in an animated manner, using exaggerated facial expressions. Or use a deadpan expression for a special effect.
- Tack an afterthought on the end of an otherwise serious statement.
- Use a surprise ending.
- Exaggerate.
- Make an intentional error.
- Use incongruities.

- Appear to let your tongue slip.
- Look for humor in real life. Some of the funniest, most entertaining stories grow out of day-to-day experience. Develop an eye and an ear for the idiosyncrasies and incongruities of everyday life.
- Avoid stories that are long and drawn out. Ruthlessly cut out extraneous words and sentences that do not move concisely toward the conclusion. Shorten the joke or story to get to the heart of the matter, or leave it out.
- Let the ham in you emerge. Acting out a story, when appropriate, makes it more interesting.

Here are some cautions to keep in mind.

- Humor should be in good taste and inoffensive. The bottom line is not simply to get a laugh, but to get a laugh without offending anyone. A good rule of thumb to follow is this: "When in doubt, leave it out."
- Avoid a sarcastic attitude.
- Don't go on and on. Remember the old saying, "Brevity is the soul of wit."
- And finally, don't make extravagant claims. Avoid saying things like "This is the funniest joke I've ever heard" or "This one will crack you up." Don't promise "funnies"; just deliver them.

Storytelling

Certainly one of the oldest forms of speaking is storytelling. Men, women, and children have always told stories, whether to a friend, at the dinner table, as part of a classroom presentation, or before an audience. Everyone loves a good story. Certainly Jesus recognized the power of storytelling in His preaching and teaching. We read in Matthew 13:34, "All these things Jesus spoke to the multitude in parables; and without a parable He did not speak to them."

Whether a story will form the whole of your presentation or be used to illustrate and help make a point within your speech, there are several things that should be kept in mind.

Selection of Material

What will be the age or ages of your audience? Will your story be the only thing on the program or will it be one of several items? Have you been allotted a certain length of time for your presentation? If it is to a part of a speech, you probably will want to either select a brief anecdote or shorten a longer story.

What kind of story would be of interest to that particular audience? If it will be made up of male children, an action-packed tale would be a good selection. For men, something to do with sports might resonate well. For the female gender, try something about people that deals with relationships. If you're not sure about a certain choice, try it out on a few people of that age or gender, or, if you don't have children of the appropriate age, borrow the offspring of a friend.

What is your purpose in telling the story? Is it just to entertain? Is it an opportunity to introduce an author the group is unfamiliar with? Do you wish to share a favorite work of literature?

Will you read the story, memorize it, or present it ad lib?

If the story features characters who speak with accents, can you pull them off effectively and maintain consistency throughout your presentation?

Here are some suggestions for making your presentation dynamic and enjoyable.

- Introduce the story you are going to tell. What kind of story is it? If it's by a known author, tell a little about the author and, perhaps, why he or she wrote it. If it's a true story, present some of the background and what happened to the leading figures after the end of the story. If it's set in a different era, give some information about what life was like at that time. If the story takes place in another country or a different state, share a little about that place, perhaps showing where it is located on a map.

- Either know the story by heart, or, if you plan to read it, know it so well that you only have to glance at the book periodically so that you can maintain eye contact with your listeners.

- If you do use a book, hold it up so that the top of the book falls just below your chin. This way your face is not hidden, but you can easily look at the page without lowering your head.

- Let the ham in you emerge. Act out the story with suitable facial expressions, vocal levels and inflections, and body language.
- Move around as appropriate. If you need to use a microphone, try to use a wireless.
- In a story with two or more characters who speak, assume a different posture for each one and give each one a distinctive voice and manner. Remove the "he says, she saids" whenever possible.
- Tell the story with animation and lots of appropriate gestures.
- Use your imagination to involve your audience. For example, for a story about animals, you could have children make an appropriate sound, such as a growl for a bear, either at your cue or whenever that animal is introduced into the story. With children, ask questions such as, "What do you think will happen to Snow White?" Or you might let some of the children show how they think the witch would walk.
- Use visual material when possible. A flannel board or hand puppets can be very effective. While we usually think of those approaches for use with children, most adults enjoy them as well. You might use a real object or objects, such as a figurine or a basket, which play a prominent part in the story.

Good storytelling takes a lot of preparation and a great deal of energy. It can be a great experience for the storyteller as well as the audience.

Dramatic Presentation

A dramatic presentation may be used in many different ways in speaking. It may form the whole performance, or it may be used as only a portion of a speech. For example, the information from the Bible about part of a character's life may become the subject for a monologue. In that case, it would be well for a different speaker to briefly introduce the character, give the setting, and, perhaps, tell a bit about what has previously happened in that character's life.

Another approach, instead of telling a story in the midst of a sermon or lesson, is to become that character and tell the story in first person from his or her perspective. This approach gives variety, adds interest, and introduces an element of surprise into the presentation.

The entire presentation may be used to portray one character, or the speaker may assume the roles of several characters. The latter approach is used in reviewing a play or a novel for a group. Note that copyright laws need to be strictly respected. Unless the play or novel is in the public domain, royalties will probably be required, even if you are not charging for the performance.

Another approach is to have someone else join you in a duet acting scene. Still another approach is to use an interview technique. For example, you might have a man dressed as Peter come down the aisle, and you could interview him about the events of the crucifixion.

Here are some suggestions for making your dramatic presentation interesting and successful:

- Memorize your presentation. The dramatic presentation cannot be given as effectively if you have to use a script or notes.

- Wear a costume, or if you are using a dramatization in the midst of your presentation, quickly don a costume piece. For example, putting on a crown when portraying royalty gives a dramatic effect and takes only a moment.

- Stage your presentation, moving around rather than staying in one spot. If you are speaking from a lectern or pulpit in a large area, you will need to use a cordless mike.

- Use appropriate gestures, vocal inflections, and facial expressions, just as you would if you were acting out a part in a play.

- If you are doing more than one part, use a different voice, posture, body language, and characterization for each character.

The following dramatic monologue, describing Queen Esther's experience in going without permission before the king, was used in the middle of a sermon titled "For Such a Time as This." A robe was quickly put on, and the part was dramatized. Afterwards, a young woman said that she had never really understood that story until she saw it acted out.

Queen Esther (based on the book of Esther, chapters 2-10)

I was extremely upset when my uncle, Mordecai, sent word inside the palace that it had been ordered that all the Jews should die. At Mordecai's direction, I had not told the king that I was a Jewess. He instructed me to go to the king and plead for the lives of my people.

Everyone knew that you did not go into the king's presence unless he called for you. Anyone who foolishly disobeyed this edict would automatically be killed—unless the king held out his golden scepter toward you.

Even though the king had made me queen, I did not have the real rank of reigning queen since I had been selected from his harem. So I knew those rules for entering the king's presence applied to me just as they did to anyone else. Besides, the king had not called for me in more than a month.

I was terribly frightened, so I sent word back to Mordecai that I could not do that. He pointed out that I would be killed with the other Jews. He also said that perhaps God had placed me in the palace for this purpose.

It was a difficult decision to make. Not only would I be risking the luxurious life I led, one that I had always dreamed of; I would be risking life itself. Finally, after much agonizing deliberation, I determined to do what had to be done. I sent word to Mordecai that, although it was strictly forbidden, I would go in to see the king. My husband, of course, was an unbeliever. I knew I would be risking everything. But I made the decision: "If I die, I die."

I asked Mordecai to get our people to fast for me for three days. At the end of the three days, I knew it was time to go in to the king.

I realized that his first sight of me would determine my life...or my death. I had to look as appealing as I possibly could. I carefully selected my most glamorous dress. My lips trembled as my maids helped me with makeup and jewelry.

My heart nearly stopped beating as I entered the beautiful inner court of the palace. There was the king, seated on the royal throne, dressed in his robes of state, glittering with gold and precious stones. He was a formidable sight. At first he did not see me. He was looking down. When his eyes met mine, I thought I would faint. I could not tell what was in his thoughts. It seemed an eternity. But finally he raised his golden scepter. He then said the most amazing thing: that I might have whatever I asked...up to half of his kingdom. My response was to invite the king and Haman—the one responsible for the order to kill the Jews—to a banquet that evening.

That afternoon was a rush of activity as the king's favorite foods and the most pleasant setting possible were prepared. It was a wonderful evening. I was careful to give him great honor. Once more the king asked what my desire was, and he promised up to half of his kingdom. I asked him to return with Haman the next evening for still another banquet.

I do not believe it was by accident that the king had trouble sleeping that evening. He decided to look over some records. There he noted that my Uncle Mordecai had warned him several months before of men who were plotting to kill him and that Mordecai had not been honored for saving the king's life.

That evening, when the king and Haman came again to dine with me, the king inquired for the third time what I would have him do. It was then that I petitioned for my life and the lives of my people.

When the king learned that Haman was responsible for the planned massacre, he had Haman executed. He honored my uncle by giving him Haman's position. I have no doubt that God placed me in the palace, protected me, and turned the king's heart toward me in order that my people might be saved.

Devotional

The devotional is an inspirational message, usually delivered toward the first part of a meeting or teaching session in order to set a positive, encouraging tone and atmosphere. It should be short— usually not more than about five minutes in length. It is an intimate type of speaking and may be quite informal in delivery.

While a devotional may take many forms, an appropriate approach is to construct one with these four main parts.

1. A scripture passage that focuses on the devotion's theme and message.

2. A story about a subject the listeners will find of interest and can relate to. Personal experiences are an excellent approach, since you don't have much time; sharing something from your own life results in instant rapport with your audience.

3. An application of the story to a spiritual principle reflected in the Scripture.

4. A short prayer that relates to the rest of the devotional. Here is a sample of a devotional developed according to that pattern.

The Parable of the Baby Duckling[4]

In all things shewing thyself a pattern of good works
(Titus 2:7).

Cici struggled out of the water and lay on the bank, looking completely exhausted and pitifully bedraggled. She had almost drowned.

We had tried to coax her into swimming a couple of times before, and she would have no part in it. Today, seeing her mother and siblings gliding effortlessly near the bank, my son had decided to toss her out near them. After all, ducks are born knowing how to swim, aren't they?

We finally figured out Cici's problem. It wasn't that she couldn't swim. She didn't know that she was a duck and that she was supposed to swim.

Cici's mother had been scared off her nest by the roar of the lawn mower one Saturday evening just as her babies were hatching. I kept looking out at her nest in the hollow of a willow by the lake in our backyard. No mama duck. Finally, about midnight, I went out and placed the newly hatched ducklings and the one remaining egg in a box and brought them into the kitchen. I was afraid a snake or raccoon might have them for a midnight snack.

Early the next morning, there was the mother duck, pacing frantically back and forth on the bank looking for her babies. I took the fluffy little peepers out to her and witnessed a happy reunion. But I kept the egg in the box. By this time, the egg was cracked, and a tiny webbed foot was emerging.

A few hours later Cici was out of the egg, waddling around. I scooped her up and took her to the bank. Her mother and the other ducklings greeted her excitedly. She immediately ran away from them, back to me. When I tried to leave, she absolutely panicked and ran frantically after me as fast as her little legs would carry her. She was so pitiful that I ended up taking her back inside with me.

Later, we learned about a phenomenon called imprinting. Ducks think the first moving creature they see is their mother. As far as Cici was concerned, I was her mother, and she was a human being...not a duck. Any time she was out of her box, she followed me around or rode on my shoulder. She wanted to be where I was and do what I did. I was her example.

All of us are examples to other people...whether or not we realize it or want to be. There are those who are looking at us as examples of what a Christian should be and do. They are patterning their lives after ours, just as Cici patterned after me. My experience with Cici prompts a searching question: Is my life a worthy example of Jesus' love and power?

Prayer: Dear Lord, make me ever mindful that, as a Christian, I am your representative wherever I go. Whether I am driving, shopping, playing, worshiping you, or working in the marketplace, there are those who are observing not only my words and actions, but also my attitudes. Help me this day, by your grace and your power, to be your worthy representative.

Pulpit Presentation

Consider: Senator Sam Ervin told about the lady who went to church and heard a young minister preach. When someone asked her what she thought of his preaching, she said: "He spoke in true apostolic style. He took a text and went everywhere preaching the gospel."[5]

Too often sermons are considered boring. Cain Hope Felder said, "In 1 Corinthians 15:31, Paul says, 'I die daily'; and too frequently the biblical usage in churches...gives new meaning to Paul's statement! Indeed, a popular, literalist, and proof-texting approach to the Bible causes many Old and New Testament personalities to die daily—week after week and Sunday after Sunday."[6]

Sermons needn't be, and certainly shouldn't be, boring. They can break out of the restrictive mold in which both preacher and congregation tend to cast them. Here's some food for thought on the subject.

- Although sermons may be short or long, popular culture seems to call for short—so that listeners can make it to the cafeteria before the crowd. But the need and setting may call for longer sermons. Time must be taken to tell the good news and the story. Since most congregations are less knowledgeable of the Bible than they were in the past, more detailed explanation is often needed.

- Sermons may be one-way—or they may be two-way, or interactive. Most people today do not like to be preached at from a person with an attitude of superiority.

- Sermons may use complex, theological jargon, which only a seminary graduate can comprehend. Or they may be cast in words and terms to which people can relate and which they can understand.

- Sermons may seek to amaze and amuse, or they may seek to engage and transform the lives of the hearers.

- Sermons may grow out of and be based on the prevailing culture, or they may use Scripture to question and confront the reigning mindset of the culture.

- The speaker may seek to be politically correct, or he may speak the gospel without fear or hesitation.

- The minister should speak the truth in love with the realization that sometimes the truth, even when spoken in love, will arouse anger and hostility.

Pulpit presentations or sermons can come in many shapes and sizes. The sermon can be written according to the same pattern as a presentation (as outlined in Chapter 7) with main points and supporting material. It also may be presented as a story with flow with the speaker's own experience or observation becoming the main vehicle from which listeners draw out the meaning.

A pulpit presentation may be developed around a spiritual topic, such as faith. Scripture passages from several books in the Bible and illustrations from the lives of biblical and contemporary people, including the speaker, would be appropriate.

Another approach is to take the life of a biblical character or story and relate it to the lives of people today. For example, the story of the deliverance of the Israelites from Egypt and their wilderness journey can be used to show how God has always worked in the lives of his people.

Some other approaches include the following:

- Use of a contemporary dramatic sketch to introduce a sermon on the subject of the sketch.
- Presentation of the entire message as a dramatic monologue (for example, a costumed depiction of Paul telling his conversion and ministry)
- A shared sermon in which two speakers interact to bring a message. Of course, in this case careful preparation must be made, and the speakers must be able to bounce off one another.
- An interview, within the sermon, with a costumed biblical character, a saint from the past, or a real missionary.
- A dramatized version of a biblical story either at the beginning of the message or within it.

One thing is for sure: regardless of the approach you use, the mission of the church—to proclaim the gospel of Jesus Christ—should not be neglected due to an emphasis on accommodating the culture. Calvin Miller expressed this point well:

The marketplace sermon should never be divorced from an honest emphasis on biblical exposition. The danger will come in trying to provide all the hooks the preacher needs to snag a secular audience. In holding the attention of the biblically illiterate, preachers will be tempted to move away from the Bible....[W]e must not water down the gospel.... [N]on-biblical preaching over time will develop only "lite" Christianity....The long-range consequence is that the church will cease to pass on its great truths to future generations.... [W]e must interest our audiences without syncretizing what the Bible teaches with other multi-cultural values.[7]

The Impromptu Speech

Consider: When faced with making a speech on the spur of the moment, remember the promise of Luke 12:12: "For the Holy Spirit will teach you in that very hour what you ought to say."

One of the most challenging types of speaking is the impromptu speech, the one you had no idea you were going to be making. Then there you are, suddenly on your feet before a group of people who are sitting there expectantly waiting for you to say something.

Don't panic. There is a way out without falling flat on your face and short of dropping dead on the spot. Here are some pointers to help you do a good job—even if you'd rather be anywhere besides standing in front of those people.

- First of all, don't apologize. Don't say that you had no idea you were going to be called on to say something. Act poised—even if you don't feel poised. Who knows? You may even fool yourself.

- Realize that the audience doesn't expect a magnificent speech on the spur of the moment. Most people aren't going to remember what you say anyway.

- Act enthusiastic about having the opportunity—even if you don't feel at all thrilled over the turn of events.

- Stall for time to get your thoughts together. If the presider asks you to say "a few words" and it's an informal group, you might get up, say slowly, "A few words," and then act as if you're going to sit down. Talk about how pleased you are to have been given this opportunity to say something to the group, or say something pleasant about the occasion. All the time you're making pleasantries, your brain can be organizing what you're going to say.

- Use the "rule of three." There's an almost magical quality about that number for a speaker. It provides mental hooks to hang your thoughts on. You can talk about three things we can do as a group, three things you would like to point out about the occasion or a certain situation, or three things you remember about the person being honored.

- Structure your thoughts around the past, present, and future. For example, talk about the tremendous contributions this organization has made in years past, what members are doing today, and how tomorrow promises to be even better.

- Use the journalistic approach. Hang your thoughts on the five Ws. Talk about who, what, why, when, where and add how for good measure. This, too, gives you a structure—something to help you organize your thinking—quickly.

Speaking off the cuff can be a stimulating, rewarding experience. The most important thing to remember is this: don't panic. When

you have to rise unexpectedly to say a few words, have confidence
that you can also rise to the occasion.

The Speech of Welcome or Greeting

The purpose of the speech of welcome is to create a warm, friendly
atmosphere for those being welcomed and to set the keynote for the
occasion. This type of speech is appropriately given for a number of
different occasions: a convention, a conference, a meeting, a special guest
or group of visitors, an occasion to honor an individual or a group, or an
occasion to welcome new members to an organization or a group.

It is a brief presentation—usually no longer than three to five
minutes. It should fit the spirit of the occasion. Although it usually
has some "fluff " and is a little on the flowery side, be sure that you
can make your remarks sincerely. A touch of humor is appropriate to
get the meeting or occasion off to a pleasant start.

The speech of welcome should contain the following elements:

- A reference to the group and occasion
- Complimentary, appreciative statements about the group or
  person being welcomed or greeted
- Facts about the place or city if participants are from out
  of town or if the meeting is being held at a historical or
  significant site
- Expression of expectation and best wishes for a successful,
  profitable meeting

Here is an example of the speech of welcome or greeting.

Welcome to Student News Conference

It's a pleasure to welcome you as a group of student journalists to
this news conference today. I have been looking forward to this
opportunity to meet with you and to interact with newspaper staff
members from various high schools.

As you very well know, writing is a tough taskmaster. I congratulate
you on your interest in this area...because, regardless of what you
may do, career-wise, writing well will be a distinct asset to you.

I heard a story about Mark Twain in his early days as a reporter that
I thought you might enjoy.

It seems that his editor harped on never stating anything as fact—not even a minute detail—unless he could verify its authenticity from personal knowledge. Well, Twain was sent to cover an important social event. He evidently had learned his lesson well, for this was the story he turned in.

"A woman using the name of Mrs. James Jones, who is reported to be one of the society leaders of the city, is said to have given what purported to be a party yesterday to a number of alleged ladies. The hostess claims to be the wife of a reputed attorney."[8]

Well, another editor's pet rule was that names must be obtained in writing all news items. He stressed over and over that names are essential. This is the story he got from a cub reporter.

"Last night lightning struck a barn northwest of town belonging to Ike Davis and killed three cows.

Their names were Rosie, Isabel and Mabel."

I think this news conference is an excellent idea, and I would like to introduce to you the lady who organized and made arrangements for it.

(Introduction) She has asked that four of us talk a few minutes about some current topics that she feels you will find interesting. She has asked me to discuss the school district's policy on the separation of church and state.

Following my presentation, _____ and _____ will talk about grading and reporting, respectively. Our final speaker will be _____. He will fill you in on recent legislation relating to student discipline.

I'll be looking forward to seeing the stories that you will be writing as a result of today's news conference. I hope you will remember to send me a copy.

The Speech of Dedication and Commemoration

The purpose of the speech of dedication or commemoration is to focus on the importance of the occasion and/or those who played a significant role in the event or project.

This type of speech is given for the dedication of a memorial, a building, or another area, such as a creative playground; a founder's day, an anniversary, or a historical event. These types of events are formal occasions, so it follows that the language of the speech and the style of delivery should also be rather formal.

The program of dedication or commemoration should contain the following elements.

- A brief welcome to the event
- Introduction of special guests, the person or family of the person being commemorated or for whom the structure is being named
- A statement of the importance of the occasion
- A review of the events leading up to the occasion
- In the case of a dedication, a summary of the use to be made of the building
- An acknowledgment of the contributions made by individuals involved in the project, such as the architect and builder
- A challenge to live up to the ideals, purposes, or heritage of the organization

Several brief speeches presenting various viewpoints are usually appropriate on such occasions. For example, the program for the dedication of a new church building might go something like this.

1. Invocation
2. Hymn
3. Welcome and introduction of special guests (pastor)
4. History of church (chairperson of governing body of the church)
5. Special music
6. Purpose of building, expressions of appreciation (denominational official)
7. Response (member or members of the congregation)
8. Closing hymn
9. Benediction
10. Reception and tour of building conducted by church members

Here is an example of a welcome speech and dedicatory remarks for a new Christian school building.

Welcome for Christian School Dedication

There's an old Spanish dicho or proverb that says: "Mas vale tarde que nunca." "Better late than never."

I know to all of you—the parents, students, staff members, and friends of_____ Christian School, this lovely new building was a very long time in coming. All of us were disappointed when construction delays due to bad weather and city inspection procedures dashed our hopes of starting the school year in this dynamic and beautiful setting. But I'm sure you will agree with me, as our dream becomes a reality today with this dedication, that this wonderful facility was well worth the wait. So I extend an enthusiastic welcome to each of you to this momentous occasion.

In the words of Walt Whitman:

"There was a child went forth every day,
And the first object he looked upon, that object he became.
And that object became part of him
for the day or a certain part of the day,
Or for many years of stretching cycles of years.
The early lilacs became part of this child,
And grass, and red and white morning glories,
and white and red clover...
And all the changes of city and country wherever he went...
They became part of that child who went forth every day,
And who now goes, and will always go forth every day."[9]

Certainly this beautiful school will continue to have a major impact on the lives, the learning, and the spiritual development of the students who study here, as well as on this entire community.

School Dedicatory Remarks

Winston Churchill said, "We mold buildings, and they then mold us."[10]

I agree wholeheartedly. I think the surroundings that we provide for our young people have a significant bearing on their motivation for learning and the effectiveness of the job our teachers can do. The surroundings also make a definitive statement about how much we value children and their future.

Certainly this beautiful building will provide an, inspiring atmosphere for _____ students. As we have watched it take shape, it has already had a positive impact on our student and community morale.

A leading psychologist says that designs of buildings and even furnishings can definitely affect personality. He offers as a prime example an employment office where new carpeting actually decreased clients' tensions. They immediately and very noticeably became considerably more cooperative and less defensive. The psychologist interpreted their response to be due to the impact of the pleasant surroundings, which made them feel positive about themselves—even though they were unemployed.

I am excited to see so many gathered here today. Seeing you tells me that you care very much about the education of these children. Certainly it is impossible for me to overemphasize the importance of that kind of involvement on the part of parents and the total community with this school.

Your participation in today's event and in school activities throughout the year makes an important statement to your children—that you believe education is important. This lovely facility also makes a positive statement—that school is a very nice and wonderful place to be.

This school is beautifully and carefully designed to meet the needs of the individual student. Several of our students will provide tours of the building after the formal part of our program today. I hope each of you will take the time to visit all parts of the building.

Someone has said, "Education is a companion which no misfortune can decrease...no crime destroy...no enemy alienate...no despotism enslave. At home, a friend...abroad, an introduction...in solitude, a solace...in society, an ornament. It chastens vice, guides virtue, and gives grace and government to genius. Education may cost financial sacrifice and mental pain, but in both money and life values, it will repay every cost one hundred fold."

As principal of _____ Christian School, it is
my very special privilege to dedicate this magnificent new facility
to these noble purposes and to the Christian principles we espouse
and seek to instill in our students.

The Commencement Speech

The purpose of the commencement speech is to congratulate
those graduating for their accomplishment and to inspire them as
they go on to greater things.

This is a formal occasion. It follows that the speech should be
rather formal in tone, but certainly not stiff or humorless. It should
be relatively short, particularly if there is a large group of graduates
who have to walk across the stage. Most graduates are too excited
to pay attention to long, drawn-out remarks; and, realistically, other
guests came to see a friend or relative receive a diploma or degree —
not to listen to a longwinded speaker. The speaker should address
not only the graduates but the other guests as well.

The commencement address should contain these elements:

- Congratulations to graduates
- Acknowledgment of the importance of the support,
  contributions, and influence of faculty, families, and friends
- Reference to the future
- Inspirational and motivational thoughts

Here is an example of a graduation speech.

High School Commencement Remarks

During the Vietnam War, American prisoners were often confined
in what were called tiger cages. Because the Communist guerillas
in South Vietnam were constantly on the move through the jungles,
they kept their POWs not in fixed prison camps, but in small
portable prisons that could be quickly picked up and moved.

In this way the tiger cage was invented. Made from bamboo
sticks, the little jails often average about five feet in length and
approximately four feet in width — obviously too small for most
American males to stretch out in.

Year after year, American prisoners of war remained cramped, crowded, and confined in these portable prisons. Can you imagine what such an experience would be like? At least one prisoner lived that way for six long years.

A Navy flier who had experienced this awful type of captivity said, "One night I succeeded in working one bamboo stick loose. That was all I needed to step out, and I was free."

Fortunately, most of us will never have that kind of experience. But how many of us build our own tiger cages and imprison ourselves in a tiger cage of the mind?

Locked within every person's mind are vast possibilities that have never had the chance to be realized. The human mind has tremendous power to dream, to visualize, and to imagine. How tragic that that potentially potent creative power is so often caged in bars of our own making and rarely allowed to stretch to the fullest degree possible.

This evening I would like to suggest three ways to remove the bamboo sticks from your mind and to release the creative power within you.

1. First of all, remove some words from your vocabulary. As graduates, you've spent more than twelve years adding to your vocabulary, but I'm here to tell you that there are some words you are better off without. One of those is the word "can't." It's one of the greatest robbers of accomplishment around. Avoid it like the plague.

I used to know a teacher who, at the beginning of the year, would write the word "can't" on the board. She would then take chalk and with a dramatic sweep cross out the "t" and say: "If you don't learn anything else in my class, I want you to remember that there's only one letter's difference between can't and can. Cross out the 't' and can't becomes can." She would go on to say that she considered can't one of the worst four-letter words around, and heaven help the student who said "I can't" in her class. She drilled that principle into them until I'm sure, even today, her students feel guilty if they use the word "can't."

Another no-no is the word "if." It's so easy to convince ourselves that we could do great things if only...If only I were smarter. If only

I had more money...or greater opportunity...or a better profile... and on and on.

Gary Gariepy of Motivation Associates says, "The little word 'if' has been the bane of mankind since the days of armed Sparta and cultural Athens. The word itself denotes a condition—and a condition denotes an uncertainty. And uncertainty implies confusion and confusion never leads to success."[11]

"If" focuses our attention on obstacles rather than on assets and positive possibilities.

2. The second bamboo-stick remover is setting definite, specific goals. Of course, just setting goals won't do the job. You can make a beautiful list of things you want to accomplish and sit looking at the list and admiring it for the rest of your life.

Think first in terms of short-range, achievable goals. Write down specific steps you will have to take to remove them from the paper and make them a reality in your life. Then set a specific date for accomplishing each one of them.

If necessary, enlist the aid of a trusted friend as your official motivator or prodder or nagger—whatever title you want to bestow—someone who will help you stay on time and on target in attaining your goals.

Be sure your goals are worthy and big enough to be challenging and exciting. Someone has said, "Aim for the moon, because if you miss, you'll still be there among the stars."

Some years ago a headline told of three hundred whales that suddenly died. The whales were pursuing sardines and found themselves marooned in a bog. The tiny fish lured the sea giants to their death. Those huge whales with vast power were chasing small, insignificant goals.

A person without goals can come to the end of life only to discover that the bulk of his or her life history can be summarized by the following statistics:

20 years sleeping,
5 years dressing and grooming,
3 years waiting on others,
1 year talking on the phone, and
6 years watching television.

Without definite, stimulating goals, the routines of life can easily become the ruts of life that lead nowhere.

3. The third bamboo-stick remover is to make up your mind that you are going to absolutely refuse to fear failure. That kind of fear can be the greatest paralyzer there is.

When you think about it, all of us have failed on numerous occasions, or we wouldn't be here this evening. All of us fell down many times in trying to learn to walk. If you play baseball, certainly you didn't hit a home run the first time you picked up a bat. In fact, heavy hitters— the ones who hit the most home runs—also strike out a lot.

Thomas Edison was once asked how it felt to be a failure after 1,200 futile attempts to invent the filament of his great dream, the incandescent light bulb. His response was significant. "I have not failed. I have discovered 1,200 materials that won't work."[12]

So often it's what a person does with what happens that spells the difference between failure and success.

Did you know that the honeybee makes her honey from exactly the same nectar with which the hermit spider distills one of the deadliest poisons known?

Julie Andrews is a good example of what I'm talking about. She played the leading lady in the Broadway hit "My Fair Lady." When Jack Warner decided to make the play into a movie, he signed up nearly all the Broadway cast with one major exception—Julie. Of course, she was disappointed. But when she was asked to star in "Mary Poppins," she accepted with relish.

At the Academy Awards, "My Fair Lady" swept the awards with one notable omission. Julie Andrews won the Oscar for her starring role in "Mary Poppins." In her acceptance speech, she said, "I would like to thank the man who made this possible—Jack Warner."

As you graduate this evening, look to the future with great anticipation and optimism. Don't allow tiger cages to surround your mind and stifle your hopes, your dreams, and your ambitions of what you can be and become.

The Speech of Tribute or Award

The purpose of the speech of tribute or award is to acknowledge and honor a person, persons, or a group for outstanding accomplishment, service, or dedication.

This type of speech is appropriately given for the following occasions: presentation of a prize, plaque, or other award in a contest; retirement or going-away party for an employee leaving a place of employment; honoring an outgoing officer of a club or other organization; banquet honoring a person for outstanding service to the community; recognition of a person performing a heroic or noble deed.

The person presenting the award should be familiar with the recipient or at least know enough about the person to make her or his remarks warm and personal. A touch of humor may be appropriate, depending on the particular situation. Cautions include the following: don't let the occasion become too sweet and syrupy to the point of embarrassing the honoree, and don't exaggerate the person's contribution or the future possibilities.

The speech of tribute should contain these elements:

- A very brief welcome to the occasion
- Pertinent information about the award or occasion
- Accomplishments and virtues of the person being honored
- Presentation

Here is an example of a speech of tribute given at an appreciation dinner for a community leader who was moving to another city.

Speech of Tribute

The Bible tells us that there is a time for all things, a time for every purpose under the heavens—a time to keep silence and a time to speak. And I am glad that today the time has come to speak about the many contributions that _____ has made to this community and its citizens.

Speaking of time,_____ reminds me of a good watch—open-faced, pure gold, quietly busy, and full of good works.

Open-faced, he is a man of commitment—to his church, to his community, to education, and to his personal convictions. I have been impressed with his integrity in standing up for what he believes—whether it's the popular stance or not.

Pure gold, he has provided stalwart leadership for the_____ _____ schools as president of the school board for the past three years and as a member for the past six years. He has provided the leadership to bring the schools through a time of great pressures and problems. Through this positive guidance, he turned what could have been crisis times into times of fertile opportunity. He has brought distinguished credit to the_____ schools as he has represented us on the state and national levels.

Quietly busy, he is unassuming and humble about his many significant contributions and outstanding accomplishments.

Full of good works, he gives unstintingly of not only his time but also of himself. He devotes what would be a full working week for most people, without any remuneration and certainly at the expense of his business and time with his family.

The people of this community owe _____ an overwhelming debt that mere words cannot convey. He has been a significant force for stability, for improvement, and for positive change. His influence and contributions will be sorely missed by all in this community.

There is a time for all things. And since he feels that it is time for him to move on to other challenges, I am honored to have this time tonight to pay tribute to an outstanding person and an effective leader. May God be with you and bless you, _____ _____, in all your future endeavors.

The Roast

The roast has become an increasingly popular way to pay tribute to a person of accomplishment and service in a lighthearted, fun-filled, tongue-in-cheek manner. Although a well-done roast is fun for everyone, it is probably one of the most difficult types of speeches to write…and to give, especially for the person not blessed with a flair for comedy.

A whole evening, complete with a dinner, is usually devoted to the roast. Since there are always several people invited to roast the honoree, remarks should be kept brief.

Some tips to use in roasting the honored one are these:

- Use exaggeration.
- Pick on a prominent physical feature or ingrained habit (but be sure it's not one the roastee is sensitive about).
- Tell a humorous incident about the honoree that really happened.
- Tell a proven joke and make the roastee the central figure.
- Make up some ludicrous, obviously untrue tale and tell it as though it actually happened.
- Eliminate any material that might offend or embarrass the honoree or anyone in the audience.
- Make stories broad enough to be obviously untrue but true enough to fit the roastee's personality and manner of operating.

Here is an example of a roast speech given for a baldheaded civic leader.

Roast

I have really been looking forward to this occasion with relish. You know, I always did like that verse in the Bible about an eye for an eye and a tooth for a tooth. And after being the roastee at the hands of_____ recently, it's good to be on the other end of the fire this time.

The only problem is that _____ has so many shining attributes, it's hard to find a flaw to focus on as you usually do when you're roasting someone. (pause) But then, of course, if you stop to think about it, one of his attributes is shinier than all the others.

In fact, this attribute got him into a lot of trouble when he was city attorney. I guess it was pretty embarrassing being in that kind of position and getting arrested. You see there were all these wrecks on Central Expressway. The Police Department was completely overwhelmed with calls. Traffic was tied up for blocks. No one could decide what was causing all the accidents. Finally they figured it out.

_____was driving down Central at noon in a convertible, and the glare from his head was blinding all the motorists. He was arrested for being a public menace.

He entered a contest once—claimed he had more hair on his head than a cue ball. (pause) The cue ball won.

But one thing I can say about _____: he's not at all sensitive about his lack of hair. He says that instead of thinking of himself as bald, he thinks of other people as hairy.

You know, I don't think many people really realize the lasting contribution_____ made to the City of _____ _____. He worked tirelessly to get some really important laws on the books. As a result of his dedicated efforts, we are now blessed with some outstanding ordinances that few cities can boast of.

For example, he put a stop to all those convict types who were feeding pigeons downtown.

Thanks to _____, the city jail is full of criminals who could not resist the urge to climb a tree in a city park.

He also made it illegal for lawless citizens to ride a bike with no hands. He put an end to citizens' herding their cattle across a public street. Now that's what I call a real contribution.

You know _____ is an outstanding lawyer, but, like every counselor at law, he took a while to get his practice cranked up and going strong.

When he first got out of law school, he opened his law office and sat there expectantly, waiting for his first client. Finally, this man walked in, and_____didn't want him to know how inexperienced he was. So he grabbed the phone and said, "No, I'm very sorry, but I can't take your case, not even for a $10,000 retainer fee. I'm just too busy."

He hung up the phone and looked at his visitor. "And now, sir, what can I do for you?" he asked briskly.

The man said, "Oh, nothing really. I just came to connect your telephone."

You may not know it, but _____ is quite an athlete. He's really an ace at tennis. Why, he even beat_____ in a big match. Of course, she had sprained both her wrists and was holding the tennis racket in her teeth...but he won.

I'll tell you one thing, though, I have really learned a lot from____ _____.

I've studied his administrative style, and it's just amazing the way he operates. I've never seen anything quite like it. It's difficult to find just the right words to describe it. But finally I realized that, as an administrator,_____ is like an iceberg— 10 percent visible, 90 percent submerged, and 100 percent at sea.

The Memorized Speech

While most speeches can be given successfully using notes, there are some types that really need to be memorized in order to be truly effective. These include the dramatic speech; the book, play, or musical review; and most stories, unless you are using a picture storybook and showing the audience the illustrations as you go.

Portions of other types of speeches should also be memorized if the presentation is to be the most effective. These include the following:

- The introduction of all speeches, in order to develop eye contact and maximum rapport with the audience
- The conclusion of all speeches, in order to end with maximum impact
- Jokes and humorous stories
- Entertaining speeches and roasts except, perhaps, for minimum notes to help keep your material in sequence. These types of speeches call for constant involvement with your audience in order to be successful. Brief notes can even be written on the palm of your hand. Just be sure not to wash your hands before you speak.
- Brief speeches, such as a speech of welcome

Suggestions

If you are doing a full-blown presentation, such as a dramatic monologue, have a copy of your material nearby. Even though you may have done this presentation many times, there's always a possibility, due to distractions such as a loud clap of thunder, that you could go blank. Or have someone follow the script in order to be able to prompt you. In case you do forget, just laugh and say something like this: "This was bound to happen sooner or later," find your place and continue. If you don't get uptight and embarrassed, the audience will hardly notice.

Memorization is an individual process. Some people find that tape recording themselves reading the entire presentation and listening to it repeatedly is quite helpful. One advantage is that you can practice along with the tape while you're driving the car. Others find that thinking of a presentation in segments works well. For example, you could use time segments of a person's life or periods of a day to help stay on track. Another approach is to keep in mind certain key words to ferry your thinking from one part of a story to the next. The important thing is to find out what works best for you.

Practice, practice, practice. Realize that it's quite different being able to say a memorized speech in the isolation of your home or office but quite a different challenge before an audience. If possible, give your presentation for one or more persons before the big event.

Another challenge in presenting a memorized speech — especially one you give over and over — is to make the material sound fresh, exciting and unmemorized. One approach is to give key portions word for word but paraphrase other parts to keep them from sounding "canned."

Being able to memorize easily is a learning process and can be a major asset for a speaker. The less dependent you are on your notes, the more you will be able to interact with your audience and the more effective you will be.

The only speeches that should be read word for word are formal position statements, policy decisions, and those with legal ramifications. Otherwise, use your notes as little as possible.

Chapter 10

CONDUCTING MEETINGS

Now therefore go, and I will be with your mouth and teach you what you shall say (Exodus 4:12).

Consider: Meetings, like certain forms of wildlife, are protected under the law. The First Amendment to the Constitution of the United States says in part that "Congress shall make no law... abridging...the right of the people peaceably to assemble." Under this guarantee, meetings seem to have multiplied like rabbits...until today it seems that everyone is on his way to or from a meeting.

Remember this simple definition of a meeting: "A meeting is a group of people who have come together for a common purpose." Of course, the challenge is seeing that the purpose is accomplished. If you are presiding at an official meeting of some type of board, of course, you will want to make certain that you are thoroughly familiar with "Robert's Rules of Order" and have minutes of what transpires in the meeting carefully recorded. In any meeting, someone should be appointed to keep notes.

One aspect of a meeting, and one that has a greater impact on the success of a meeting than most people might imagine, is the meeting room itself and the way it's arranged.

These are some considerations.

- Lighting should be bright enough for people to write but not so bright that there's a glare. Can the lighting level be controlled?

- Acoustics should be such that speakers can be easily heard all over the room. Carpet helps acoustics. It also is easier on the feet for a presenter or chairperson who will be standing most of the meeting. It is better not to use microphones unless they are absolutely necessary. They tend to inhibit some people and can slow down a meeting if a person has to change location in order to speak.

- Are heating and cooling adequate and reliable?
- Are there enough electrical outlets conveniently located?
- Are adequate speaker's stands, tables, etc., available?
- Dry-erase boards on stands are sturdier than those on an easel. Black markers are best for readability.
- A room without windows protects from distractions.
- Posts should not obstruct vision.
- Select the proper room size. Allow about eight hundred square feet for thirty people with tables and chairs, about one thousand square feet for fifty people.

Seating Arrangements

One of the most important things to consider is how to arrange seating for a particular type of meeting. The closer the participants are to the presenter or presider, the better. It is also easier to generate interaction, enthusiasm, cohesiveness, motivation, and team spirit when members of the group are seated close together. For this reason, it's a good idea to use narrow tables.

A good rule of thumb is to set up for about ten percent fewer people than you expect to come. It's always better to add more chairs than to have too many empty seats.

Here are some good arrangements for meetings.

These arrangements encourage good group interaction.

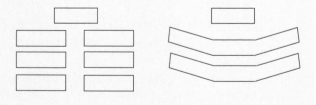

(about twenty maximum)

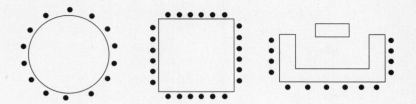

And this arrangement facilitates small groups within a group interaction.

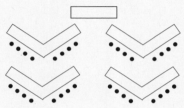

Conducting Effective Business Meetings

Consider: Business meetings can be expensive to your organization in terms of man hours and can turn into endless bores that accomplish little unless they are well planned and run smoothly. The following suggestions should help keep a meeting on time and on target.

Prior to Calling a Meeting:

1. Ask yourself, "Is this meeting really necessary?"
    *   Consider other possibilities.
    *   Try a conference call to see if an agreement can be reached by phone.
    *   Write a memo outlining the issue and asking for a response to a proposed solution by a certain date.
    *   Try to consolidate discussion with an already scheduled meeting.

2. Keep the meeting as small as possible by inviting only those who will be making the decisions.

3. Clearly define the purpose of the meeting and let participants know in advance exactly what is to be accomplished.

CHECKLIST FOR PLANNING MEETINGS

Prior to the meeting
Publicity
___ Notices
___ Letters of invitation
___ Bulletin boards
___ Personal contacts
___ News release (if apropos)

Agenda
___ Plan agenda
___ Plan for involvement
___ Contact people on agenda
___ Previous minutes
___ Committee reports
___ Materials needed

Space and Equipment
___ Place reserved
___ Equipment reserved

Just before the meeting
Space
___ Room arrangement
___ Seating arrangement
___ Extra chairs
___ Climate control

Equipment and Supplies
___ AV equipment set, checked
___ Extension cords
___ Microphones
___ Gavel, felt pens, pencils, pads
___ Newsprint
___ Visual aids
___ Agenda, other handouts
___ Name tags

At the meeting
___ Meeting, greeting, seating participants, guests
___ Greeting and seating latecomers
___ Handing out materials
___ Operation of equipment
___ Recording meeting

End of meeting...and after
___ Collect unused materials
___ Return equipment
___ Clean up
___ Thank helpers
___ Read and analyze evaluation, feedback
___ Remind people of follow-up commitments
___ Plan for next meeting: set date, etc.
___ Send minutes to participants

4. Send out an agenda in advance with the most important item at the top.

5. Set a time limit for the entire meeting and for each agenda item, and stick to it.

6. Schedule the meeting before lunch, another meeting, or an engagement to help ensure that the meeting will end on time.

7. Select an appropriate room for the size and makeup of the group.

8. See that the room is arranged for optimum interaction. The closer the group sits to one another, the easier it is to generate enthusiasm, cohesiveness, and motivation.

9. Consider several alternative solutions prior to the meeting and develop backup information, costs, and possible outcomes for each possibility.

10. Figure up how much the meeting will cost the company in salaries, etc., per hour.

During the Meeting:

1. Start on time regardless of who is missing.

2. Assign someone to take notes and keep time on each agenda item.

3. Clearly define the purpose of the meeting.

4. Stick with the agenda.

5. Limit interruptions to emergencies.

6. Restate conclusions for clear understanding and to ensure a commitment of purpose.

7. Make assignments with due dates clearly stated.

8. End on time.

After the Meeting:

1. Send notes of meeting, listing assignments and due dates, to participants and any other staff members affected by the decisions.

2. Follow up with progress reports on implementation of decisions.

3. Have each participant turn in an evaluation of the meeting.

MEETING EVALUATION FORM
(Please check the appropriate answer.)

___ yes ___ no   Did you feel this meeting was necessary?

___ yes ___ no   Was the purpose of the meeting clearly defined?

___ yes ___ no   Did you receive a copy of the agenda before the meeting?

___ yes ___ no   Did you receive backup materials to study in advance of the meeting?

___ yes ___ no   Was adequate attention given to answering questions?

___ yes ___ no   Did the meeting start on time?

___ yes ___ no   Was the agenda followed?

___ yes ___ no   Was the purpose of the meeting accomplished?

___ yes ___ no   Were conclusions summarized accurately?

___ yes ___ no   Were assignments made clearly?

___ yes ___ no   Were realistic time frames set for completion of assignments?

___ yes ___ no   Was the meeting room suitable and appropriately arranged?

What suggestions would you make to improve future meetings?

Brainstorming

Consider: Brainstorming is probably the best technique available to get a group of people communicating and working effectively together. It breaks down barriers in rank and often results in some excellent, workable strategies for solving a problem or for implementing a new thrust or program.

The purpose of brainstorming is to obtain as many ideas as possible in a given time period. Quantity is welcomed. No idea is to be discussed or judged. It is absolutely forbidden for anyone to grimace, make a negative comment, or put down another's idea.

A large group may be divided into several smaller groups of seven or eight persons. Each group can work on the same project and, afterward, share its results with the other groups. Or each group may be assigned a different aspect of the project, so that an overall plan may be developed. In the case of multiple brainstorming groups, each group should be given the opportunity to present its completed portion of the plan to the whole gathering at the end of the session. In a meeting on communicating with employees, for example, one group might discuss effective ways to communicate with office personnel, another effective ways to communicate with maintenance and custodial workers, and a third effective ways to communicate with professional employees.

Appoint someone in the group to record the ideas. Have the recorder write them with a felt pen on big sheets of newsprint or on a dry-erase board so all group members may see them.

Instructions to Facilitator(s)

- Briefly explain the topic, problem, or goal for the brainstorming session. Go over the ground rules for brainstorming.

- Limit the size of the group to about seven or eight participants. In a larger group, divide into smaller groups for brainstorming.

- Give participants two or three minutes to ponder the subject and think of several ideas.

- Go around the table and have one participant at a time state an idea in a short, complete sentence.

- Make sure all ideas are recorded.

- Don't allow any criticism or discussion of any idea.

- Canvas the group as many times as needed to encourage participants to express all their ideas. Participants may pass when they run out of ideas.

- Arrange for ideas to be typed in a list or written on a smaller piece of paper if they're to be the object of additional discussions later in the same session.

- Arrange for any ideas participants may have after the session to be added to the list. Often participants will get their best ideas after a session is over.

Ranking

- When participants have the complete lists at hand, ask each member to rank the five suggestions they feel are the best, from one (for the top rating) down through five. Ranking may also be done by a show of hands when the ideas are still on the newsprint or dry-erase board.

- Compile the individual rankings to derive the group's ranking of the best ideas.

- Discuss the best ideas for reaching the stated goal or solving a certain problem.

- One idea may be selected as the very best and a plan of action developed from it.

- If more than one small group has brainstormed, get the whole group back together and have a member of each group report on what they came up with.

Advantages

- Since all ideas are welcomed, regardless of merit, all members feel they may participate as equals.

- A great number of ideas can surface in a short time, and some are sure to be worth considering.

- There is no time-wasting discussion of the merits of all ideas.

- Participants will start to bounce off each other with one's ideas sparking a new idea in someone else.

- Brainstorming is an excellent vehicle to develop rapport among members of a group and a great way to get acquainted.

Handling Types of Participants in Meetings

Consider: you will find basically two groups of participants in meetings: those who are eager to talk and those who don't want to talk at all. Trying to involve the non-talkers and to keep the talkative ones from dominating a discussion is a real art, requiring great diplomacy and skill. As a presider, it is important and to your advantage to remain cool and collected at all times and to treat participants with dignity—even if they are being rude and contentious.

Types of Participants	**Solution**
Ax grinders	Discuss the situation if it fits the subject under discussion. Otherwise, indicate an interest in the person's problem and offer to discuss it after the meeting.
Non-stop talkers	Interrupt when they take a breath and summarize what's been said. Then ask someone else a question. If they persist, turn the attention of the group toward someone else by saying, for example, "Jim might have some insight into this question."
Blasé Brendas and aloof Als	Try to tie the discussion into their area of expertise or experience. Ask them to share their wisdom or experience on the subject.
Racial or political expounders	State firmly that those particular issues cannot be discussed in this meeting.
Whisperers	Stop talking and look at the individuals. Ask one of them a question or for an opinion.
Illogical concluders	Say, for example, "That's an interesting perspective."
Stubborn standers	Recognize that they may not really understand the issue under discussion or its ramifications. Get them to expand on their point of disagreement. Restate your premise. Get others to help you explain. Or, as a last resort, offer to discuss the question with them later.

Participant's Behavior	**Solution**
Contentious spirits	Try to ignore their comments by pretending not to hear them. Recognize any legitimate complaints. Offer to discuss the matter with them after the meeting. Assign someone who has responsibility in the area of their complaint to talk with them privately about the problem or concern. Often the group will help you take care of an obvious troublemaker. As a last resort, take them aside and try to enlist their cooperation.
Silent Sams and Samanthas	Ask them a direct, provocative question.
Participants arguing among themselves	Interrupt with a direct question. Bring other audience members into the discussion. Ask that the discussion be limited to the facts.
Strayers from the subject	Say, "Someday perhaps we can talk about that, but right now we need to finish our discussion on...."
Poor Speakers	Recognize that they may have great ideas but are limited by fear or vocabulary. Restate their contribution by saying something like this: "In other words, you think ...."
Radicals	Say in a pleasant tone of voice, "Well, of course, you're entitled to your opinion."

Participant's Behavior	**Solution**
Eager answerers	A person who always wants to answer first can easily sabotage your efforts to involve as many persons as possible in the discussion, especially if they blurt out the answer without being recognized. A good way to handle such a person is to say, "After I discuss this question, I'm going to ask _____ to summarize what's been said."
Shrinking violets	Ask direct questions you are sure they can answer. Ask if they agree with a statement. Comment favorably if they do get the courage to contribute.
Ramblers	When they come up for breath, thank them, rephrase one of their statements, and call on someone else or go on to the next topic.

Guaranteed Snafus for Meetings

Keep members waiting. As chairperson, arrive on time...and then start getting ready for the meeting. At the next meeting, more members will arrive late, assuming that the meeting will not begin on time anyway.

Do all the planning yourself. People are more likely to support what they feel they have had a part in planning and carrying out. Ask others for suggestions, advice on how to improve future meetings, or let a committee assist with the planning.

Conduct every meeting exactly the same way—without variation. While some people cling to routine, most people find it monotonous over a long period of time. Add a little festivity occasionally by moving to a more glamorous setting or by serving some really interesting refreshments.

Fail to plan for the best arrangement of the room. A classroom-style seating arrangement is not conducive to group discussion. Decide in advance what will work most effectively for this particular meeting.

Assume that equipment is working properly and that audiovisual material can be seen and heard. Probably nothing is more irritating to an audience than mechanical failures and illegible or inaudible media approaches.

Assume that everyone knows the purpose of the meeting. The goal or goals of the meeting should be stated clearly when the meeting is called and at the beginning of the meeting.

Don't have a prepared agenda. Discussing whatever comes up is a sure way to lose the interest and support of the very people who are the most important to your success. A prepared agenda helps keep the meeting on track and gives you something to point to when members stray from the subject.

Let a few people hog the meeting. Some of your best insights and suggestions may come from members who are not aggressive enough to shout down incessant talkers. It's up to the chairperson to ensure that each person present has an opportunity to contribute.

Fail to have notes taken at the meeting. A summary of the meeting is important for future reference and in making sure that assigned tasks are being carried out by the due dates. A copy of the minutes should be sent to all those present, to members who were unable to attend, and to others affected by the decisions or plans.

Don't have a definite time to end the meeting. Most people are simply too busy to attend meetings that drone on and on. They want to know how long the meeting is scheduled to last, and they want to know that they definitely will be through at that time.

Chapter 11

SO, YOU'RE GOING TO BE ON TELEVISION

*Let them shout from the top of the mountains…. And declare
His praise in the coastlands (Isaiah 42:11b, 12b).*

Consider: Appearing on television is definitely a different type of experience from speaking in front of an audience. Few people have the opportunity to become acquainted with this unique environment before actually being thrown into it.

The following tips may be useful if you suddenly find you're going to be an interviewee on a television program.

What to Wear

As a rule, television will make people look several pounds heavier than they actually are. An outfit that is slenderizing can be a real plus. Solid colors for major items of clothing, such as a suit or dress, are safest. Big, bold patterns are distracting and call attention away from the interviewee. It's better to shy away from bright white. Pastel colors are safer for, say, a man's shirt. Avoid wearing fabrics of high sheen. Lightweight clothing will be much more comfortable under the bright lights.

Shiny jewelry should be avoided, as should any jewelry that might make a noise, such as a charm bracelet. A necklace or tie clasp could also cause problems by hitting a lavaliere microphone or the microphone cord.

Men should wear socks that cover the calf. These eliminate the possibility of an ankle's shining forth if legs are crossed. Also, socks should match the pants. Remove items such as wallets, glass cases, and keys from your pockets.

Consider how your outfit will look when you're seated. For example, a short, tight skirt on a woman can be a disaster on screen. Simplicity is an excellent rule to follow.

How to Prepare

Watch the show you'll be appearing on, several times if possible. In this way you'll gain a feel for the format, the type of questions the host usually asks, and the overall tone of the program.

If you're not accustomed to bright lights, consider talking at home with the brightest lights you can find shining in your eyes.

If you're going to be interviewed, ask a friend or relative to practice with you as the interviewer until you become thoroughly at ease with that format and sound conversational.

If you need statistics or direct quotes, print or type these on individual index cards.

If you have any kind of visual material you would like to use, check it out with the program host well in advance of the program. As a rule, it's better to have the material or object set up somewhere in the studio rather than to try to hold it steady on camera.

Arrive early for the interview. Doing this gives you the opportunity to become familiar with your surroundings and, perhaps, the chance to discuss your interview in greater depth with the program host.

During the Production

Be sure to make clothing adjustments as needed before the session begins. Men will usually need to pull coats down in back, because they tend to hike up on the neck when seated.

Always look at the person you're talking to. Make eye contact with the person who is interviewing you. If you're in a group discussion and someone else is speaking, give that person your undivided attention.

If you wish to address the viewer, look directly into the camera. For example, if you are representing a charity drive, your host might give you the opportunity to make a direct appeal for funds to the viewing audience. Or, if you are giving a solo presentation, of course, you would look at the camera.

Try to be as natural and conversational in tone as possible.

Keep your shoulders parallel to the floor and your head up straight. Otherwise, you'll appear to be a listing vessel.

Although gestures are fine, be on guard against sudden, darting movements. Pity the poor director who has a tight close-up of your face and sees it suddenly disappear from view.

Be sure not to touch the microphone or its cord.

Time cues will be agreed upon before the show begins. Although time is the responsibility of the production staff and your host rather than you as a guest, you need to be sure not to get into a long, involved explanation when there's only a minute left in your segment of the show. If you don't understand the question, don't hesitate to ask for clarification.

If an untrue statement is made, refute it diplomatically.

If you are asked a series of questions, pick the one you most want to answer and give that information first.

Some Cautions

Unless you're accustomed to using a teleprompter (in the case of some type of prepared statement or use of quoted material), don't attempt it. Using a teleprompter smoothly takes a lot of practice and can be disastrous when done awkwardly.

Once the program begins, assume your microphone is on at all times. If you don't want something broadcast, don't say it.

Never look off the set, regardless of what happens. Resist the temptation to be distracted by what the production crew is doing.

Concentrate completely on the interview.

A special warning should be heeded about looking at the studio monitor. There have been occasions when guests have gotten so fascinated by watching themselves on the monitor that they completely lost contact with what was happening in the interview.

Be sure to keep your language simple, especially if you're talking about a technical subject. Assume that your listener knows little or nothing about your field.

Don't become bogged down in a string of statistics or a long, drawn-out explanation. You'll lose your viewer.

Always remain seated until you are told you may leave the set. Watch those chairs! If you're seated in a swivel chair, don't swivel. One with rollers can be disastrous, especially if you're seated on a platform.

Don't ever assume you're off camera, even when others are

speaking. The director may decide to come to you for a reaction shot at the very moment you scratch your nose.

The Reporter Cometh[1]

The usual interview program is quite different from being interviewed in an emergency situation. The following information will help you to be prepared in case you suddenly find yourself confronted by a television reporter holding a microphone in your face and demanding information about an emergency situation.

Being prepared means knowing what to expect from the media and the way in which to respond that will be most advantageous in a crisis. Once a crisis occurs, the news media will be close on its heels. And they will not be put off. The reporters have been given an assignment. Their job depends on their getting in a story by deadline.

Saying, "No comment" or "I'll meet with you when I have more information" won't work. If you won't talk, they will get their information from someone who will—someone who may give opinion rather than fact or someone who has an ax to grind. If the media can't get something from the "horse's mouth," they will get something from somebody in time to meet their deadline. Here's the point to remember: it is far better to have accurate information from a top official than to have rumors quoted from an outside source.

When an emergency situation occurs, it's a waste of time to quarrel with a reporter by saying something like this: "I can't imagine why you're interested in this," or "Why don't you spend time explaining why millions of tax dollars are wasted by outlandish government spending rather than on this triviality?"

The reporter really doesn't care what you think of a story being done. His or her job is to get the assigned story, and the reporter will probably become very irritated by those kinds of comments.

Hassling the reporter, claiming no knowledge, or minimizing the situation will make the reporter suspect that you're hiding something. Refusing to return a reporter's calls will irritate her or him and usually result in a more damaging story.

If you are an official spokesperson, it is to your advantage to give the facts as you know them. Then state that you are looking into the situation and will hold a news conference at a certain time later that day. The reporter knows that an incident did occur, that the situation is under control, that you are not attempting to cover it up, that you know the importance of an immediate response, and that more information will be given at a specific time. This information gives him or her something to report and you time to plan for the news conference.

News Conferences Provide Opportunities

At the news conference, give the information as you know it to be. Details that have not been completely verified should be prefaced with the phrases "as we have been able to ascertain so far" or "at this point, we believe...."

Give the steps that your organization plans to take to rectify the problem or to keep the public appraised of the situation. For example, if your church has been destroyed by fire, try to give the location where Sunday services will be held. Make it a point to work in as many positive elements as possible—such as the quick-thinking and heroic efforts of workers in evacuating the young children from the building.

Donald W. Blohowiak, author of *No Comment! An Executive's Essential Guide to the News Media*, gives the following advice:

> Reveal bad news in total. The slow drip, drip, drip of damaging facts piques public interest and surrounds the story in an air of a drama unfolding....[R]evealing all there is to tell right off the bat allows the media to tell everything in one shot. The resulting bang may be deafening for a brief moment, but then it's in one ear, out the other, and quickly forgotten in the face of noise from other news events.[2]

In a controversial situation, avoid giving the reporters the opportunity to keep the story going over several days or even longer. You do not want them to keep coming back and prolonging and enlarging on the story. A one-time negative story is not nearly as damaging as one that is reported at several points and by an increasing number of stations and newspapers. Telling about a plausible plan to rectify a problem may dim the reporters' interest in a return visit.

Respond in an Interview to Your Best Advantage

Becoming familiar with the news media in your area and how they operate, before a crisis occurs, will give you a distinct advantage.

What are the reputations and records of the stations and newspapers you might conceivably deal with? Who are their audiences? Who are the reporters who might logically be assigned to cover a story about your organization? Would they be familiar with your group?

If you've worked in advance to establish credible media relations on an ongoing basis, you have a distinct head start in dealing with the media in a crisis. Julia Duinn, a writer for newspapers for more than a decade, suggests, "Know whom you are dealing with." She points out that, according to the survey of media attitudes conducted by Lichter-Rothman, reporters are far more liberal than are the people they report on.[3]

Showing news persons respect as professionals who are doing a difficult job will usually result in their showing respect for you as a professional who is also performing a challenging job.

Decide What You Want to Say

First, pick the spot for the interview that will be most advantageous to you. Have in mind an alternative setting in case there is too much glare, noise, or other distraction in your first choice of location.

Then decide what is the overriding message that you want to get across. Try to frame a statement in one sentence that will tell your story. You may even want to write it down and memorize it so you can speak smoothly and with confidence. Don't assume that the reporter will ask the right questions so that you can present the information you desire. Having a clear, concise statement already prepared will help you weave it into the interview.

Be aware that the anchor's introduction of the story and the reporter's comments will probably take up most of the time allowed for that particular report. There may be room for only one sentence from you as an interviewee. Be sure it says in a nutshell what you want to leave with the listener.

Anticipate Possible Questions

Cast yourself in the reporter's role and ask yourself what questions you would want answered about this particular story. Ask a colleague to help you brainstorm possibilities. Focus on the line of questioning that might come from a reporter who is not well informed or from an aggressive type who may ask abrasive and probing questions. Be prepared to field each question with a brief, well thought-out reply.

Help the Reporter Understand the Situation

Remember, your best protection against an erroneous, slanted story is a reporter who fully understands the situation. He or she may be new to your city or may not know any of the background. Assume that the reporter is rather ignorant on the subject. It is better to be too basic than to assume knowledge that isn't there. Keep in mind that silence is not a good option, for it can appear that you have something to hide.

Use Set-up Time to Good Advantage

Even if the reporter and videographer appear rushed, they have to take time to get ready for the interview. As the person being interviewed, you can use that time to good advantage by talking in a friendly manner with the reporter. What you say during those few minutes can help plant ideas in her or his mind that will lead to questions that will allow you to say what you desire.

Also, be cordial to the videographer. Although the reporter is in charge, the videographer also can influence the outcome of the television interview. Too often the interviewee ignores the videographer as though he or she is only part of the equipment. But remember that the videographer determines the camera angle to shoot and whether to use an extreme close up. Probably, too, the reporter will discuss the story with the videographer on the ride back to the studio.

Sometimes, if the reporter has to go cover another story, the videographer will decide how the story should be edited. Learn and use both their names.

Be Conversational in Tone and Use Simple Language

You do not want your replies to sound as though you are giving some kind of oration. Neither do you want your response to sound as though it is coming out of a textbook. Think of the interview as an opportunity to go into the citizen's living room and explain your situation or point of view.

Remember that a news interview is not the place to display your excellent vocabulary. Newspapers are written on an eighth-grade reading level for a reason—so that everyone can understand them. A reporter will not use your reply if it is couched in language that is over the head of the average person. Rather, you will find your words rephrased in the final story in simpler terms by the reporter. It is especially important to avoid using acronyms and jargon. Use words and terms that communicate your message precisely and concisely to the average person.

Be Enthusiastic and Spontaneous

People will be much more interested in what you have to say if your words and facial expressions are a matching pair. A deadpan expression is boring and turns viewers off. Also, be aware that a shot of you with the voice of the reporter over the picture may be used when you are not even speaking. Or you may be speaking, but your volume may be lowered while the reporter tells the story.

Though your responses may be well prepared, they must appear to be spontaneous. The way you say what you want to share may be as important as or more important than what you say.

Look at the Reporter and Leave the Microphone Alone

Never look directly into the camera in a news interview situation. It looks unnatural, awkward, and even shifty to the viewer, especially if the interviewee looks back and forth from the reporter to the camera lens.

The reporter will position the microphone in front of you for your reply. Resist any temptation to reach out and take it or even touch it. The reporter is not about to let you hold it. At worst, it may come off looking as if you are in a physical struggle for possession of the microphone.

It is the reporter's responsibility to make certain that the audio is being recorded at the proper level. That responsibility, of course, involves knowing the type of microphone and the distance it should be from the interviewee's mouth.

Remember that Honesty Is the Best Policy

It is far better to admit to an error or mistake than to try to cover it up. Reporters seem to take great delight in exposing lies and misrepresentations. The next couple of examples back up the wisdom of going the honest route. Not only reporters but also the public seem to respect the integrity of someone who admits, "I was wrong."

When President John F. Kennedy acknowledged his responsibility for the Bay of Pigs fiasco, polls showed that his popularity did not wane. In fact, it went up ten percent.

Several years ago Ford Motor Company recalled thousands of Montego automobiles because of faulty axles. The Ford Company was not sure what the impact would be. Apparently, though, the buying public appreciated the company's diligence in not risking the safety of its automobile owners. After that event, sales rose seventy-seven percent.

If you or your group made a mistake, present a plan for rectifying the error. Also, admitting a mistake removes the controversy, and the story may well die a natural death at that point. Not admitting to an error will usually result in deeper probing and more media attention. That tactic also can get you on a reporter's "hit list," which is not a good place to be.

Get to the Point Concisely

Chances are your interview for television news will last from three to five minutes. After the interview is edited, the story may last only about thirty seconds, and your statement will be even shorter. You may end up with only one or two sentences from the entire interview in the story. The reporter may talk over a sentence in your interview leaving only a part of the sentence of your actual words. So you see you do not have the luxury of being expansive and elaborative on a statement. Make your point with the fewest words possible.

Bridge from the Question to What You Want to Say

Even though the reporter chooses and directs the questions, remember that you control the answers. You can briefly answer the question and, in the same sentence, expand the topic to include the message you want to put across. You can say something along the lines of the following statements:

"but it is important to remember...."

"and that reminds me of...."

"While that is a problem, this is what we are doing to try to solve it...."

"Of course this is a challenge, but it's no greater than one we've successfully met in the past."

Turn the Question

If the question is one that you do not want to answer, don't answer it, but in a pleasant way that is not offensive. You can respond with statements like these:

"I don't really see that as the main issue here. The main issue is...."

"I would have thought your question would be...." Then proceed to answer it.

"I think most people are more interested in..., and, of course, that's what we're concentrating on here."

Buy Time to Think of an Answer

If you are taken off guard by a question, stall for time in order to come up with a good answer. For example, ask the reporter to repeat the question. Or tell the reporter that you want to be sure that you understand the question. Rephrase it and ask him or her whether that is the correct interpretation. During this exchange, you will have a good chance to order your thoughts.

Remember Who the Real Audience Is

While you are talking with a reporter, remember that your real audience is not the reporter. The listener or viewer is the person toward whom your message is directed. Don't think about that one individual with the microphone but rather about the public and what you want it to know. Your goal is to get beyond the "human filter" and reach the reporter's audience.

Avoid Answering Ranking Questions too Specifically

If a reporter tries to pin you down to your number-one priority or major concern, you would do well to hedge the question by making it more inclusive. You might counter, "Well, of course, we have several important priorities. Among these are...." Then discuss one or two.

Use the Reporter's Name in an Important Statement

Reporters are human, too. They like to have their name within the report as well as at the end. It makes them seem to be well-known and respected in their field. Addressing the reporter by name gives you a better chance of getting your priority statement included in the story.

Realize that the Reporter May Know Something You Don't

If the reporter brings up something you are not aware of or an accusation someone has made, be careful in your response. Be prepared to say, for example, "I am not aware of a problem in that area," or "I will be glad to look into that."

Sometimes a reporter may have a predetermined mindset about the situation. In the case of an obviously erroneous belief on the part of the reporter, the person being interviewed must be convincing, so as to overcome the inability of the reporter to grasp the truth.

You might confront the reporter with an empathizing phrase: "That's difficult to believe, isn't it?" or "That trend's been dead for several years." Or an even more forceful response may help. You could say, for instance, "Your story may already be written, but I don't believe it's complete." Try to force a mental turnabout. Then back up your statement with solid facts, background, and reasons to drop the original hypothesis.

Do not allow a reporter to put you on the defensive. Be bold, ensuring that you present proactive elements of the story. If the reporter surprises you with rumors, say, for example, "I don't know about the rumors, but I do know...."

Remember These Don'ts:

- Avoid responding by saying "No comment" or "Talk to my lawyer," especially if the camera is already rolling. That kind of statement will almost certainly be used on that evening's news, particularly if you are scowling or shaking your fist at the reporter. Those types of replies put you in an adversarial role and make it appear that you have something to hide. It is better to be unavailable for comment, especially if you do not wish to be interviewed. If, in the case of a matter under litigation, your attorney has instructed you not to speak on the subject, make that explanation politely and with an apology as though you really wish you could oblige the reporter with an interview.

- Don't question the reporter's motive. Doing so only leads to the media's questioning your motives. Ken Muir, a school information director, considers two questions in deciding whether to release information. The first one is this: "Why should I not provide this information?" He says that those who ask instead, "Why should I?" can always come up with a lot of lame excuses. The second question is this: "If the questioner were to go to court to get this information, would he win?" If the answer is yes, Muir says, you might as well give it gracefully and save yourself a lot of headaches.[4]

- Don't clam up. Remember that silence can be damning. A reporter will usually try to present both sides of the story. The Fairness Doctrine stated, "Broadcasters are charged by the Federal Communications Commission with the affirmative duty to seek out and broadcast contrasting viewpoints on controversial issues of public importance." Although this doctrine is no longer in effect, many media outlets still abide by its principle. If only one side is available for comment, that side, of course, is the only one the public will hear. It is almost always better to present your case.

- Don't ever become hostile. Unfortunately, there are television reporters who try to goad an interviewee into losing her or his temper, making an angry response, or becoming belligerent. Though that reaction might be justified in light of the provocation, the viewer, doubtless, will never know it. The questions, in all likelihood, will be cut, leaving the interviewee looking like some type of maniac. The interviewee has everything to gain and nothing to lose by responding consistently with politeness and restraint.

- Don't make any remarks "off the record." Assume that any statement you might make will be used. There may be a misunderstanding about what you designate as "off the record." Even if there is a firm off-the-record agreement, your remark may tip the reporter to an unknown bit of information. The reporter probably can then find someone else to interview and get the same facts. Play it safe and do not say anything that might come back to haunt you. Also, be aware that when a radio reporter calls for a telephone interview, the tape may already be rolling. Any flippant remark may end up on the air.

- Don't be evasive. The importance of at least appearing to be open and above board cannot be overemphasized. An experienced reporter will hone in quickly on an area that appears to be upsetting or sensitive to the interviewee.

- Don't give just a yes or no answer. Provide some additional information. Not only does this response make for a more interesting interview; it also gives you an opportunity to elaborate on a point. Sometimes a reporter will ask a loaded question and try to get only a yes or no response. Dr. Richard M. Adams, as director of the School Health Services for the Dallas schools, shared his surefire method for guaranteeing that he has the opportunity to explain a one-word answer. "I always say, 'I would have to answer that with a qualified yes or a qualified no.' Invariably the reporter will ask, 'What do you mean by a qualified yes?' Then I get to tell more. It works every time."[5]

- Avoid saying, "I don't know." Even if you don't know the answer, it is better to present some other response. For example, say something like this: "We're checking on that right now," or "I will have that information for you later today."

- Don't walk away. It is better to stay and face the reporter in a positive manner. You may be able to override the impact of the story with your response. The reporter who is counting on negative reaction may decide that there really is not an interesting story there after all.

In brief, when a crisis does occur, remember the following:

- Respond quickly.
- Don't deny what happened or be evasive.
- Have the highest official possible respond.
- Explain openly that information is being gathered and will be available at a specific time.
- Use media time to present your side of the story with positive facts that cast a more favorable light on your group.

- Prompt positive follow-up stories. If the emergency is a major incident for your town, the media will not let it be over in one day's news cycle. It will, in all likelihood, produce numerous features and side stories for readers, listeners, and viewers.

- Be sure you don't play favorites by giving information to one reporter and not to all of them.

Chapter 12

GETTING ORGANIZED AS A SPEAKER

Being confident of this very thing, that He who has begun a
good work in you will complete it until the day of Jesus Christ
(Philippians 1:6).

Setting Goals as a Speaker

Consider: Becoming an effective public speaker doesn't just happen overnight. It takes effort, experience, and action.

Once you've made the decision to become the best public speaker you can possibly be, you can turn that desire into a reality a lot quicker by developing some definite goals. The following steps for setting and attaining goals are good ones to take to help you reach your destination. Even if you're a good speaker, this process can help you to become even better.

1. Write down the goals you want to reach in speaking, making them as specific as possible. Don't just say your goal is "to be an excellent speaker." List the areas in which you need to improve. For example, a goal might be to eliminate all filler sounds—such as "er," "uh," "you know"— from your speaking. Often, those with this ingrained habit are not aware just how many times those sounds interrupt their flow of words. If your speech will not be taped, take along a small tape recorder you can unobtrusively start at the beginning of your presentation.

2. Rank goals in priority. Which one is most important to reaching your overall goal?

3. Write down obstacles to reaching each goal and develop a concise, step-by-step plan for overcoming each one.

4. Develop a realistic time frame for reaching each step of your goal. Set aside so much time each week for that purpose.

5. Picture yourself positively completing each goal.

6. Make yourself accountable to someone else (if that's what it takes) for completing each step on time. It's great if you have a friend who is also working toward improving speaking skills and you can make a pact to monitor, encourage, and critique one another. Or make yourself accountable to God. Doing this can be a real motivator.

Let's take an example. Say you decide that you need greater vocal range, better breath control, and more self-confidence. You decide on this order of priorities:

1. More self-confidence
2. Better breath control
3. Greater vocal range

In analyzing the situation, you determine that you're never going to gain more confidence as a speaker without a lot of practice before an audience. Your plan might include the following parts:

• Speak at every opportunity.

• Make your own opportunities by volunteering to give a report or running for a club office that entails speaking, such as program chairperson.

• Join Toastmasters International.

Your plan for developing better breath control might look something like this:

• Set aside a minimum of ten minutes each day to practice breathing exercises. (Some are listed in Chapter 4.)

• Improve overall physical condition by exercising at least three times each week.

• On a regular schedule, read a certain passage into a tape recorder. Compare the breath support, endurance, and sound with your last reading.

Your steps to developing a wider vocal range could include the following:

- Set aside at least ten minutes a day to do vocal exercises. (Some are included in Chapter 4.)
- Use the tape recorder to read a passage and a piano or pitch pipe to determine your speaking range.
- Record the same passage each week and compare the range with the previous week's effort.

Your time frame might be to increase your speaking range by at least one note in a month's time.

Finding Material

Where can you find good material to use as a speaker? The answer is just about anywhere...and everywhere. Once you become attuned to seeing good illustrations and anecdotes in your everyday life, you'll be amazed at what you come up with.

Always carry a notepad with you to jot down incidents you observe, hear about, or experience. Some of the very best illustrations are simple, everyday happenings that all of us as human beings can relate to. And sharing something from your own experience creates a personal bond with your audience.

Keep your pen poised and your eye out for the following:

- Conversations between children
- Stories on television and radio
- News stories
- Material used by other speakers
- Good examples in books and articles
- Catchy phrases, unusual ways of saying something
- Examples from your personal history and that of your friends and family
- Stories that friends forward to you through e-mail

Helpful Publications

There are a number of excellent book collections of material for speakers, including several geared especially to the speaking needs of Christian speakers. There are also several periodicals designed for public speakers.

These are some magazines and newsletters that have proven to be worthwhile.

American Demographics
Crain Communications
6th Floor
360 N. Michigan Ave.
Chicago, IL 60601

Pulpit Resource
Logos Productions Inc.
6160 Carmen Avenue E
Inner Grove Heights, MN 55076-4422

Christian Communicator
American Christian Writers
P.O. Box 110390
Nashville, TN 37222-0390

Speaker's Idea File
Ragan Communications, Inc.
212 W. Superior St.
Suite 200
Chicago, IL 60610

Vital Speeches of the Day
City News Publishing Co.
389 Johnnie Dobbs Blvd. # C
Mt. Pleasant, SC 29464

There are also some organizations that you will find can help you perfect your art as a speaker.

Toastmasters International provides a weekly or biweekly opportunity for members to practice and improve their speaking skills. Most communities of any size have at least one chapter. Here's the address if you want to find out about a club in your area.

World Headquarters of
Toastmasters International
P.O. Box 9052
Mission Viejo, CA 92690

Two other organizations for speakers are these:

World Speakers Assoc.
7102 Mardyke Lane
Indianapolis, IN 46226

The National Speakers Assoc.
1500 S. Priest Dr.
Tempe, AZ 85281

Setting Up a Quotation and Anecdote File

Once your collection of material starts growing, you need to develop an organized method for keeping and locating all those great stories and other material.

Some people find that storing them by categories in a computer works well for them. Others prefer having hard copies. In that case, probably your best bet is to put each anecdote, or quotation, on an 8 1/2" x 5 1/2" file card with the name of the general topic in the upper right-hand corner of each card. Then, you can gather the cards with all the material you might be interested in using and arrange them and rearrange them in a logical order.

The real challenge is deciding on the appropriate categories— narrow enough to help in locating the material, broad enough so that you don't end up with 1,000 categories.

Place the name of each file category on tab cards and place them in card file boxes on shelves conveniently close to your speechwriting area. It's also helpful to make a list of all your categories so that you can check at a glance for a category in which you may have filed a certain item.

Although books on speechwriting contain material divided by categories, they won't match your categories. You'll save a lot of time in the long run if you go through the books and put the stories you like in your own file.

Developing Topical Files

Besides your card file, you as a speaker will also want to start collecting material, in your special areas of speaking interest, which is too long to place on cards. This practice is especially important to you if you are a frequent speaker in your career field or profession or are a Bible teacher.

Get in the habit of saving magazine articles, newspaper clippings, and copies of parts of books. Enlist the help of your friends and colleagues in looking for material in your areas of special interest.

Your local public library can be very helpful in researching a particular topic. Even if the library doesn't have the material you need, it can often be obtained from another library through Interlibrary Loan, usually at no cost. The library at a nearby seminary can be most helpful in researching spiritual topics, and most offer an outside borrower's card for a reasonable annual fee. But don't overlook other local resources that can help you localize a particular issue. These include the local chamber of commerce, charitable institutions, state highway departments, and city departments such as the city manager's office and police department. Of course, the Internet is a virtual treasure trove of information on almost any subject you can imagine.

It is important to give credit to an author or source for any major material that is used.

Light Openers

"I was invited to speak because they wanted something light with no message...and I came highly recommended."

"Someone has said that the writer of Psalm 91 must have been speaking at a luncheon club when he wrote about 'the destruction that wasteth at noon day.' Perhaps he referred to banquets when he spoke of 'the pestilence that walketh in darkness.'"[1]

"My wife (or husband) told me the other day that now she knows why I'm always asked to speak after dinner. She had just read a doctor's report that said the sense of hearing is considerably dulled by eating, and she decided that was nature's way of protecting people against after-dinner speakers."

"As I stand before you, I recognize that you come from many walks of life, that you are different people, motivated by sometimes vastly different preoccupations. But you do have one important concern that agitates you, one question for which you all seek an answer: 'How long will this speech last?'"

"The ladies' (or the men's) room at work has one of those hot-air contraptions for drying your hands. I went in there the other day, and someone had neatly written on the button that activates the hot air: 'Press here for a message from the company president' (or whatever your position is)."

"As pastor (or your role), I'm called on to speak quite often. My wife (or husband) says I get up so often that I'm living proof of the old adage that hot air always rises."

"I asked your chairperson what I should speak about, and he (or she) said, 'About 20 minutes.'"

"My job, as I understand it, is to talk to you. Your job, as I understand it, is to listen. If you finish before I do, just hold up your hand."

"You know, _____ is quite a persuasive person. A few months ago she (or he) called to tell me about this wonderful meeting. She said, 'You believe in the goals of our organization, don't you?' I said, 'You know I do.' Then she said, 'You like to share your thoughts with others, right?' I said, 'Sure, who doesn't?' She said, 'And you believe strongly in free speech, don't you?' I said, 'Of course I do.' She said, 'Good. How about coming out and giving one?' So here I am."

"Confucius once said that speaking to an audience of highly intelligent people is like eating soup with chopsticks. It's easier to stir things up than to satisfy the appetite. Today I hope to accomplish both things—to stir up your interest in _____ _____ and to satisfy your appetite on the subject."

"I am delighted to be with you today. Now I know a lot of speakers say that, but after struggling with a very austere budget until I've felt like I was wrestling with a 500-pound marshmallow, spending what seemed like a century in federal court, and having to face unexpected financial shortfalls all spring, you just don't know how happy I am to be here instead of in my office."

"It's a special privilege to welcome this group of brave people to_____. I say "brave" because I think that anyone who works day in and day out with middle school students (or whatever the group does) must either be brave or crazy, and, of course, I prefer to think of you as brave."

"At my first scheduled lecture, I caused quite a lot of comment. I didn't show up. I received one get well card and seventy-nine thank you notes."

On Being Invited Back to Speak to the Same Group

"At first I was flattered to be asked back again, but then I remembered that _____ used to be a teacher and was probably going to make me keep doing it until I get it right."

"At first I was flattered about being invited back a second time, that is, until my wife (or husband) told me you were probably trying to find out if I'd improved any as a speaker since I was here last."

SPEAKING ENGAGEMENT INFORMATION FORM

Engagement: _____ Occasion: _____

Contact: _____ Phone #: _____

Place: _____ Time: _____ Date: _____

Address and directions to location: _____

_____

_____

Audience: _____

Appropriate dress: _____

Topic: _____

Length of presentation: _____

Other speakers: _____

Checklist of items to take:

___ Reading glasses   ___ Handkerchief

___ Cough drops   ___ Notes

___ Extra index cards   ___Copy of introduction for presider

___ Props: ___ Handouts

___ Audiovisual equipment (supplies, extra bulbs)

On Responding to a Flattering Introduction

"First, I'd like to ask for a copy of that introduction. Then, the next time anyone asks, 'Who do you think you are?'...am I going to have an answer!"

"It's awfully nice to have those things said about a fellow without his family having to go to the trouble and expense of having a funeral."

"Would you mind repeating that introduction? I'd like to tape it so my congregation (or boss or whoever) can listen to it."

"That generous introduction reminds me of the man who raised his head up out of the grave on Judgment Day and read the glowing words on his headstone. He shook his head in disbelief and said, 'Either somebody is a terrible liar, or they put me in the wrong hole.'"

On Being Honored

"This is a moment I wish my parents were here to share. My father would have enjoyed what you so generously said about me. And my mother would have believed it."[2]—Lyndon B. Johnson

"I appreciate your honoring me with this very wonderful occasion. It makes me think of what Jack Benny said once when he was being honored: 'I really don't deserve this honor. But then I have arthritis, and I don't deserve that either.'"[3]

On Being Asked to Give an Impromptu Speech

"This unexpected opportunity reminds me of Jonah's admonition to the whale. (Looking at the person who asked him to speak) If you had kept your big mouth closed, I wouldn't be in this predicament now."

Appendix 1: Review

After making a speech one day, Sir Winston Churchill was asked, "Doesn't it thrill you, Mr. Churchill, to know that every time you make a speech, the hall is packed to overflowing?" Churchill replied, "It is quite flattering. But whenever I feel too flattered, I always remember that if—instead of making a political speech—I were being hanged, the crowd would be twice as big."[1]

Then there was Socrates, the first public speaker. They poisoned him.

Those two little anecdotes are included just to remind us that there are hazards in being a public speaker. But to minimize them and make sure you don't risk life and limb when you open your mouth, keep the following in mind.

A Dozen Don'ts for Public Speakers

1. Don't accept a speaking engagement on short notice unless it's a subject you're thoroughly familiar with and have spoken on before. If you're not given adequate time to prepare, it's better to turn down a request than to leave the audience with the impression that you are an ineffective, ill-prepared speaker.

2. Don't ignore the time and place of the presentation. Find out as much as possible about the setting of your speech. Is it after a meal? Who precedes you? Who makes the introduction? How is the room arranged?

3. Don't use jokes just because they're funny. A story that interrupts the audience's train of thought does not build rapport; it distracts. Unless the funny story or line helps make your point, it's better to skip it.

4. Don't fail to rehearse. Even if you're a seasoned speaker, you'll do a better job if you take the time to go over your speech from beginning to end several times.

5. Don't try to show how much you know. The quickest way to lose an audience is to use complex material and data that are difficult to understand and are filled with jargon. Remember to KISS (Keep it simple, speaker). Be sure you're on the same wavelength with your audience.

6. Don't try to dazzle your audience with a stream of visuals. Visual material used judiciously and professionally can help get across your point and focus your audience's attention. But visuals also can become a distraction if they're done poorly, if the same approach is used excessively, or if you're uncomfortable or inefficient in using them. Using audiovisual material effectively takes practice.

7. Don't assume you can handle any question if a question-and-answer period is to follow. Prepare in advance by writing down any question you think the group might ask and formulating your answer in advance. The person who asked you to speak can also suggest what may be on the minds of the people you'll be addressing.

8. Don't ignore your allotted time. It isn't fair to the audience or to the next speaker. A maximum for the usual speech is about 20 to 25 minutes. If you're asked to speak longer, say an hour, you'll need some type of audience involvement activities.

9. Don't arrive just in time to give your talk. You need to get there in time to get the "lay of the land." Early arrival gives you the opportunity to feel the mood of the audience and a chance to pick up some last bits of helpful information.

10. Don't disregard the makeup of the audience. Make sure your speech is slanted in the direction of the audience's interests, desires, and level of understanding.

11. Don't fail to define clearly the response you want from your audience to what you have to say. You should be able to state your specific objective in one sentence.

12. Don't just "be yourself." While your public speaking should be in keeping with your own style and personality, you have to be more than your usual self. You really can't

just speak in a conversational manner and keep your audience's attention. Remember, in a speaking situation, you're the whole show, and you have to be livelier and more animated than usual.

Appendix 2: Speaking the Scriptures with Impact and Power

What an exciting privilege it is to stand before a congregation and speak forth the Word of God! And what a responsibility!

I recently heard a definition of Scripture that really resonated with me. "Scripture is God present with us." And then there's a saying that reads, "The Bible is the only book whose author is always present when you read it." As proclaimers of the Word in a church service, our goal is to help the congregation experience God's presence.

Consider these Scriptures:

John 5:39: You search the scriptures because you think that in them you have eternal life; and it is they that testify on my behalf.

Romans 15:4: For whatever was written in former days was written for our instruction, so that by steadfastness and by the encouragement of the scriptures we might have hope.

What Is Our Mission, Our Purpose in Presenting Scripture?

1. To make Scripture jump off the page and leap to life for the listeners. It is no longer just words in a book written centuries ago. It becomes God present with them.

2. To testify on God's behalf. Think of yourself as appearing in a court of law. You are giving important, life-changing testimony. You are a witness of what you know to be true, of what you have seen and experienced in your own life.

3. To bring encouragement and hope. Certainly in today's uncertain economy and strife-ridden world, we all are seeking encouragement and hope. After September 11, church attendance rose. People are seeking reassurance and meaning in their lives.

4. To bring the listener into the story. By dynamically presenting the Word, we open the door for the hearers and invite them inside to participate, to take ownership of the story and make it their own.

5. To help people discover themselves in the story. Too often, I believe, people think, "Well, those people lived thousands of years ago. They didn't face the problems I do today. What do they have to do with me?" The truth is that they and we experience the basic challenges faced by every human being who ever walked the face of the earth. Our job is to make the stories pertinent to lives in the 21st century.

6. To make it seem like it's happening now—as breaking news. We hear television news anchors say, "Now a breaking news story." They try to make it sound exciting, fresh, up-to-the-minute. We want the Bible to be today's news.

7. To paint a verbal portrait of the Divine. We become word artists, showing what God is like—His nature, His love, His faithfulness. We help them to see Jesus.

That's a tall order. How can we possibly do all that?

Things to Consider

1. What literary genre are you reading? Poetry, such as the Psalms? History, such as in Exodus? Prophecy, such as parts of Isaiah? A short story, such as Ruth? An anecdote, such as one of Jesus' parables? You don't read one of Elizabeth Barrett Browning's sonnets the same way you tell a story. You don't relate a historical incident the same way you would tell about something that happened at work last week.

2. What was the author's purpose in writing the passage? Try to get inside the writer's head. Why did he choose that particular genre to express his meaning?

3. Use a commentary in order to understand the entire meaning, setting, and ramifications of the passage.

4. Read the passages preceding and following the scripture. What happened before? What led up to the events of your passage? What happened afterwards?

5. Of course, it goes without saying that you look up difficult names to learn how to pronounce them. But it is also important to repeat them until your tongue feels comfortable saying them and they become a natural part of your vocabulary.

6. Practice aloud—several times. Be thoroughly familiar with the passage so that you can look out at the congregation periodically.

Tools We Have to Work with During the Presentation

- Loudness and softness. A louder voice—or a very soft voice— can provide emphasis to a certain word or phrase. Certainly the variety helps to make it more interesting.

- Tone of voice. Express the tenderness, strife, love, bitterness of the story through vocal tone. Just about every human situation imaginable is covered in the Bible. Some are joyous, some sad, some triumphant, some funny. Others are actually shocking. Every time I read about God's having Hosea marry a prostitute and telling Isaiah to run naked through the streets, I am shocked. If I just read matter-of-factly that God told his prophet to marry a whore, it sounds as though making such a command might be something God does on a regular basis. I need to read such passages with a shocked tone of voice that says, "Can you believe that?"

- Intensity. A passage of conflict that rises to a climax, for example, is enhanced by an increase in intensity.

- Pitch. Most of us have a much wider vocal range in speaking than we ever use. A lower voice, for example, in presenting a prophetic word or the words of God can be very effective. Also, in a dialogue passage, use a slightly higher pitch for one character, then lower the pitch for another.

- Pace. Increasing the rapidity of speech can add interest and variety to any passage. An especially profound thought or conclusion can be given emphasis by being read more slowly. Or, suspense and excitement may be created by reading faster.

- Silence. An especially effective technique is the "pregnant pause." Set a word or phrase apart by pausing before and after for greater emphasis.

- Sound of a word to express its meaning. There are many words that can be spoken in such a way as to help the listener experience their meaning. For example, try saying the words "compassion," "sorrow," "wailing," "shining," or "awesome" to capture their connotation.
- Facial expressions. Practice with a mirror to make sure your facial expressions are a matching pair with the words you are speaking.
- Body language. Of course, you are not going to make elaborate gestures. But you can lean forward or back a bit and, in a dialogue, assume a slightly different body position for the two people speaking.

As presenters of the Word today, we need to realize that we may very well be speaking to those who are totally unfamiliar with the Bible. They may come from a different religious background—or from none at all. But whether they are seekers or staunch saints of long-standing, our assignment is to bring the Word of God to life and help them make it an integral part of their lives. What a privilege! And what a responsibility!

Endnotes

Chapter 1 - "Jesus as a Speaker—Our Example"

1. Herman Harrell Horne, *Teaching Techniques of Jesus* (Grand Rapids, Mich.: Kregel Publications, 1982), p. 96.

2. Joan Lyon Gibbons, "A Psychological Exploration of Jesus' Use of Questions as an Interpersonal Mode of Communication," a dissertation (Berkeley, Calif.: Graduate Theological Union, 1979), pp. 30-38. The eight types of questions Gibbons identified are these: location of an opposite, introduction of a comparison, first half of a comparison, second half of a comparison, use of hearer's experience to evoke a known side of a similarity or opposite, reference to religious tradition, a challenge to current behavior, and alternatives leading to a choice or decision.

3. Gibbons, p. 37.

4. A. E. Baker, *The Teaching of Jesus for Daily Life* (London: Eyre and Spottiswoode, 1933), p. 7.

5. Roy B. Zuck, *Teaching as Jesus Taught* (Grand Rapids, Mich.: Baker Books, 1995), p. 307.

6. Zuck, p. 324.

7. Harry Emerson Fosdick, *The Manhood of the Master* (New York: The Association Press, 1958), p. 16.

8. William E. Phipps, *The Wisdom and Wit of Rabbi Jesus* (Louisville: Westminster/John Knox Press, 1993), p. 88.

9. Elton Trueblood, *The Humor of Christ* (New York: Harper & Row, Publishers, 1964), p. 54.

10. Trueblood, p. 55.

Chapter 2 - "Making Friends with Your Worst Enemy—You!"

1. Walt Kelly, "Pogo" comic strip, *The New York Post*, Hall Syndicate, 1970.

2. Max D. Isaacson, speech given February 1, 1980, in Des Moines, IA.

3. *The Sunday Times*, London, October 7, 1973.

4. Jacob M. Braude, *Braude's Handbook of Stories for Toastmasters and Speakers* (Englewood Cliffs, NJ: Prentice-Hall, Inc., 1957).

5. James C. Humes, *Podium Humor* (New York: Harper & Row, Publishers, 1975).

6. "7 Biggest Mistakes Business Presenters Make and How to Avoid Them," booklet published by Decker Communications.

7. Quoted by Scot Morris and Nicolas Charney in "Stop It! Scaring Off Stage Fright," *Psychology Today*, July 1983.

8. Frank Swiatek in "How to Speak Before a Group," a Learning Dynamics workshop, in San Francisco, February 1984.

9. Quoted by William Safire and Leonard Safir, *Good Advice* (New York: Times Books, 1982).

10. Source unknown.

11. Dr. Boino Kiveloff, *Prevention Magazine*.

12. Quoted by Dale Carnegie, *The Quick and Easy Way to Effective Speaking* (New York: Pocket Books, 1962).

13. Ralph Waldo Emerson, *The Conduct of Life* (South Orange, NJ: Power Publisher, 1860).

14. James C. Humes, *Speaker's Treasury of Anecdotes About the Famous* (New York: Harper & Row Publishers, 1978).

15. James C. Humes, *Churchill, Speaker of the Century* (Briarcliff Manor, NY: Stein and Day, 1980).

Chapter 3 - "Presenting Yourself as a Speaker"

1. "The Act of Listening," *The Royal Bank of Canada Monthly Letter*, January 1979.

2. *Speechwriter's Newsletter*, February 19, 1982.

3. *Quote*, as reported in "Quality Circle Digest."

4. *Effective Business Communications*, Zig Ziglar Corporation.

Chapter 4 - The Mechanics of Speaking

1. *Effective Business Communications*, Zig Ziglar Corporation.

2. Quoted in *Decker Communications Report*, May/June 1983.

3. Oleda Baker, *How to Renovate Yourself from Head to Toe* (Garden City, NY: Doubleday & Co., Inc., 1980).

4. Edward J. Hegarty, *How to Talk Your Way to the Top* (Englewood Cliffs, NJ: Reward Books, 1973).

5. James MacLachlan, "What People Really Think of Fast Talkers," *Psychology Today*, November 1979.

6. Quoted by Dorothy Uris, *Say It Again* (New York: E. P. Dutton, 1979).

7. Quoted by Jacob M. Braude, *Braude's Handbook of Stories for Toastmasters and Speakers* (Englewood Cliff, NJ: Prentice-Hall, Inc., 1957).

8. Dorothy Sarnoff, *Speech Can Change Your Life* (Garden City, NY: Doubleday & Co., 1970).

9. *Speechwriter's Newsletter*, January 1, 1982.

10. Quoted by Joey Adams, *Joey Adams' Encyclopedia of Humor* (New York: The Bobbs-Merrill Company, Inc., 1968).

11. John F. Kennedy, Inaugural Address, Washington, DC, January 20, 1961.

12. J. F. Bere, "Second American Revolution," *Vital Speeches*, January 15, 1978.

13. U.S. Circuit Judge Abner J. Mikva in a commencement address at the Chicago-Kent College of Law.

14. Dr. Martin Luther King, Jr., "I Have a Dream," speech in Washington, DC, 1963.

Chapter 5 - Connecting with Your Audience

1. Laurie Rozakis, *The Complete Idiot's Guide to Speaking in Public with Confidence* (New York: Alpha Books, 1995), p. 51.

2. Mark Twain, as quoted by Winston E. Jones, *Preaching and the Dramatic Arts* (New York: Macmillan, 1948), p. 61.

3. Rozakis, p. 96.

4. Harvey Minkoff, ed., *Approaches to the Bible—The Test of Bible Review* (Washington, DC: Biblical Archaeology Society, 1994), p. 273.

5. Ibid.

6. Alice Mathews, "He Said, She Heard," *Leadership*, Fall 1995, p. 49.

7. Ibid.

8. Mathews, pp. 50-51.

9. Muriel Larson, "You Can Sharpen Your Speaking Skills," *Discipleship Journal*, Issue 22, 1964, p. 12.

10. Roy Alexander, *Power Speech—The Quickest Route to Business and Personal Success* (New York: Amacom, 1986), p. 48.

11. Jerry Vines, *Effective Sermon Delivery* (Chicago: Moody Press, 1986), p. 88.

12. George Barna, "The Pulpit-meister: Preaching to the New Majority," *Preaching*, January/February 1997, p. 12.

13. Barna, p. 13.

14. Barna, p. 11.

15. Oscar Wilde, quoted by James C. Humes, *Podium Humor* (New York: Harper & Row Publishers, 1975).

16. Bob Orben, "Bridging the Gap with Humor," *Communications Briefings*, November 1983.

17. G. K. Chesterton, quoted by Humes.

18. Sir Noel Coward, quoted by William Safire and Leonard Safir, *Good Advice* (New York: Times Books, 1982).

19. Elsa Maxwell, quoted by Leonard Spinrad and Thelma Spinrad, *Speaker's Lifetime Library* (West Nyack, NY: Parker Publishing Co., Inc., 1979).

20. Bob Hope, quoted in *Effective Business Communications*, The Zig Ziglar Corporation.

21. Roger P. Wilcox, quoted in *Effective Business Communications*.

22. Alan H. Monroe, quoted by Orben.

23. Josh McDowell, "Syllabus on Communication and Persuasion" (mimeographed, 1983), p. 18.

24. E. B. White, source unknown.

25. Orben.

26. Quoted by Sylvia Porter in Chatelaine, Canada.

Chapter 6 - Show and Tell Your Audience

1. "3M How-To Guide," 3M Corporation (nd).

2. Bell and Howell Corporation (source not known).

3. Reported by Harold Freeman, *Variety in Biblical Preaching* (Waco, TX: Word Books, 1987), p. 166.

4. Russ Olmon and Paul Avery in an interview by Wanda Vassallo, October 29, 1998.

5. Francis Anfuso, in his production manual entitled "Taking Your Church Off Pause," noted that a public-performance license is required to show motion pictures released in home video format during activities such as youth-activity programs, adult-education sessions, or general church functions. He wrote, "This legal requirement applies equally to profit and nonprofit organizations, regardless of whether an admission fee is charged." See Francis Anfuso, "Taking Your Church Off Pause" (Yuba City, Calif.: 21st Century Ministries, 1993), p. 146.

6. Jeff Burger, *Multimedia for Decision Makers—A Business Primer* (New York: Addison-Wesley, 1995), p. 115.

7. Burger, pp. 115-16.

8. Burger, p. 116.

Chapter 7 - Writing the Speech

1. Roy Alexander, *Power Speech, The Quickest Route to Business and Personal Success* (New York: Amacom, 1986), p. 49.

2. Jacob M. Braude, *Speaker's Encyclopedia* (Englewood Cliffs, NJ: Prentice-Hall, Inc., 1955).

3. Quoted in *Effective Business Communications*, The Zig Ziglar Corporation.

4. Laurie Rozakis, *The Complete Idiot's Guide to Speaking in Public with Confidence* (New York: Alpha Books, 1995), p. 97.

5. Martin Thielen, "Beyond Infosermons," *Leadership*, Winter 1994, pp. 39-40.

6. William J. Bausch, *Story Telling the Word—Homilies and How to Write Them* (Mystic, Conn.: Twenty-third Publications, 1996), p. 90.

Chapter 8 - Getting Ready for the Big Event

1. Evan Esar, *20,000 Quips and Quotes* (Garden City, NY: Doubleday and Co., 1968).

2. M. Dale Baughman, *Teacher's Treasury of Stories for Every Occasion* (Englewood Cliffs, NJ: Prentice-Hall, Inc., 1958).

3. Quoted by Herbert V. Prochnow and Herbert V. Prochnow, Jr., *The Public Speaker's Treasure Chest* (New York: Harper and Row, Publishers, 1964).

4. Lawrence M. Briggs, *The Master Guide for Speakers* (Minneapolis: T. S. Denison and Company, 1956).

5. Quoted by Bill Adler, *The Churchill Wit* (New York: Coward-McCann, Inc., 1965).

6. Quoted by James C. Humes, *Churchill, Speaker of the Century* (Briarcliff Manor, NY: Stein and Day, 1980).

7. Herbert V. Prochnow, *Toastmaster's Quips and Stories* (New York: Sterling Publishing Co., 1982).

8. Jenkin Lloyd Jones, source unknown.

Chapter 9 - "Types of Speeches"

1. Jacob M. Braude, *Speaker's Desk Book of Quips, Quotes and Anecdotes* (Englewood Cliffs, NJ: Prentice-Hall, Inc., 1963).

2. *Communications Briefings*, Volume 1, Number 1.

3. David Rees, "Being Serious About Humor," *The Clergy Journal*, Mar. 1997, p. 5.

4. Wanda Vassallo, "The Parable of the Baby Duckling," *A Parable a Day Keeps the Devil at Bay*. (Wilson, NC: Star Books, Inc., 1989), pp. 26-27.

5. Quoted in *The Preacher Joke Book: Religious Anecdotes from the Oral Tradition*, Loyal Jones, ed. (Little Rock: August House, 1989), p. 25.

6. Cain Hope Felder, *Troubling Biblical Waters—Race, Class, and Family* (Maryknoll, NY: Orbis Books, 1989), p. 79.

7. Calvin Miller, *Marketplace Preaching* (Grand Rapids, MI.: Baker Books, 1995), pp. 42-45.

8. Joey Adams, *Joey Adams' Encyclopedia of Humor* (New York: The Bobbs-Merrill Company, Inc. 1968).

9. Walt Whitman, "There Was a Child Went Forth" from "Autumn Rivulets," *Leaves of Grass*, 6th edition, 1881.

10. Quoted by James C. Humes, *Churchill, Speaker of the Century* (Briarcliff Manor, NY: Stein and Day, 1980).

11. Gary Gariepy, source unknown.

12. Quoted by James C. Humes, *Speaker's Treasury of Anecdotes about the Famous* (New York: Harper and Row, Publishers, 1978).

Chapter 11 - "So You're Going to Be on Television"

1. This information on communicating in a crisis is adapted from *Church Communications Handbook* by Wanda Vassallo (Grand Rapids, MI.: Kregel Publications, 1998), pp. 239-51.

2. Donald W. Blohowiak, *No Comment! An Executive's Essential Guide to the News Media* (New York: Praeger, 1987), p. 147.

3. Julia Duin, "How To Beat Media Phobia," *Ministries Today* (March/April 1992), p. 55.

4. Ken Muir, quoted in "Why Would You Want to Know That?" *Trends for the Secondary School*, 1974.

5. Richard M. Adams, M.D., interview by the author, Dallas, TX., 1985.

Chapter 12 - "Getting Organized As a Speaker"

1. Charles F. Banning, in *Church Management*, quoted by Herbert V. Prochnow and Herbert V. Prochnow, Jr., *The Public Speaker's Treasure Chest*, Harper & Row, Publishers, 1964.

2. Lyndon B. Johnson, on receiving the honorary Doctor of Laws degree from Baylor University, Waco, TX, 1965.

3. *Effective Business Communications*, The Zig Ziglar Corporation.

Appendix 1: Review

1. James C. Humes, *Churchill, Speaker of the Century* (Briarcliff Manor, NY: Stein and Day, 1980).

Index

A

Acoustics, 62, 80, 177
Alexander, Roy, 66
Anaphora, 15
Andrews, Julie, 170
Anecdotes, 8, 39, 63, 74, 78, 122
Apologize, 23, 25, 161
Appearance, 28, 30-31
    comfort, 18, 28
    dress, 18, 28-30, 39
    jewelry, 29, 155, 189
    men, 29, 31, 189-90
    women, 29, 31
Aristotle, 84
Audience, 4, 15-16, 59-84, 107
    age, 67, 80, 90, 126, 144, 152
    analysis, 63-73
    attitudes, 69
    background, 63-69
    comfort, 2, 24, 65, 75, 144
    common ground, 59-61, 63
    education, 65-67
    ethnicity, 63
    eye contact, 22, 28, 31, 35-37, 75
    gender, 2, 64-65, 190
    humor, 11-2, 39, 71, 75, 77-81, 113, 145, 148-51
    involvement, 59, 73-77, 89, 110, 175, 214
    occupations, 64-67
    participation, 61, 74-77
    profile, 68
    relating, 2
    special interests, 4-5, 67
Audience Analysis Form, 70
Audiovisual aids, 61, 85-103
    Biblical accounts of, 85-87
    computer-controlled presentations, 89-90
    dry-erase board, 97-98
    flannel board, 99-100
    flip chart, 98-99
    guidelines for use, 88-89
    handouts, 101-02
    hook-and-loop board, 99-100
    magnet board, 99-100
    microphone, 100-01
    movies, film, 96
    objects 87, 92-93, 100, 153
    overhead projector, 91-92, 102
    slide projector, 94-95
    sound, 93-94
    television, 97
Audiovisual Checklist, 103
Avery, Paul, 92

B

Bacall, Lauren, 43-44
Barna, George, 67
Bausch, William J., 115
Beekman, John, 64

Benny, Jack, 211
Bere, J. F., 56
Bits and Pieces, 206
Blohowiak, Donald W., 193
Body language, 27, 32, 35, 72,
    82-83, 153-154, 220
Bonhoeffer, Dietrich, 113-14
Brainstorming, 182-83
Breath control, 48-50, 204
Breathing, 17-19, 29, 48-50
    abdominal, 49
    clavicular, 49
    diaphragmatic, 49
        benefits, 49-50
        practicing, 49-50
    thoracic, 49
    types of, 49
Burger, Jeff, 89

C

Chesterton, G. K., 79
Churchill, Winston, 26, 106,
    132-33, 165, 213
Cohan, George M., 54
Colloquialisms, 69
Commemoration speech, 163-64
    examples, 165-67
Commencement speech, 167
    example, 167-71
Computer-controlled
    presentations, 89-91
Conclusion to speech, 108,
    125, 175
Coward, Noel, 79

D

David, 4
Dedication speech, 163-64
    examples, 165-67
Delivery rate, 47
    varying, 42, 45, 47
Demosthenes, 30
Devotional, 156-57
    example, 157-58
Diction, 48, 50-53
    improving, 51-53
    mispronounced words, 51-52
Don'ts for reporter interviews,
    199-201
Douglass, Mac, 43
Dramatic presentation, 153-54
    example, 154-56
Dry-erase board, 61, 72, 76, 89,
    97-98, 178, 183
Duinn, Julia, 194

E

Eating, 22, 41-42
Edison, Thomas, 170
Eisenhower, Dwight D., 21
Elizabeth, 3
Embolalia, 15
Emcee, *see Master of
    ceremonies*
Emerson, Ralph Waldo, 25
Energy, 17-19, 22, 41, 43, 46, 48
Entertaining speech, 148-51, 175
Enunciation, improving, 50-51
Ervin, Sam, 158
Esther, 154
Examples, several to make the
    same point, 8-9
Eye contact, 22, 27, 31, 35-37,
    39, 75, 152, 175, 190
    avoiding, 35, 37

benefits, 36
glancing, 36-37
moving, 37
points to remember, 36
while reading, 37
with notes or script, 37

F

Facial expressions, 34-37, 153-154
Fear of speaking, 15-16
Felder, Cain Hope, 158
Filler sounds, 53-54, 203
Film, 89, 92, 96-97
Flannel boards, 99-100, 153
Flip chart, 61, 72, 76, 98-99, 133
Fosdick, Harry Emerson, 11

G

Gariepy, Gary, 169
Gestures, 19, 27-28, 32-35, 39,
    78, 101, 133, 153-54, 191
  benefits, 33
  hands, 33
  how to use, 34-35
  roles played in using, 33
Gibbons, Joan Lyon, 6-7
Glanz, Fred, 42
Glasses, 29, 210
Glover, Terrot, 11
Goals, 124, 169-70, 188, 203

H

Haman, 155-56
Handouts, 101-02, 146
Harrison, William Henry, 62
Hawks, Howard, 43
Hegarty, Edward J., 46
Holmes, Oliver Wendell, 53
Hook-and-loop board, 99-100

Hope, Bob, 77
Hubbard, E., 16
Humor, 39, 71, 75, 77-81
  Jesus' use of, 11-12
  relevance, 78
  timing, 77
  types, 78

I

Illustrated sermon, 10
Impact of Jesus' speaking, 13
Impromptu speech, 2, 160-62, 211
Inattention, signs of and
    remedies, 71-72
Information, how processed, 27,
    48, 67
Informative speech, 145-46
International Platform
    Association, The, 207
Introduction of a speaker, 140-41
  Speech of Introduction
      Outline Form, 142
  writing your own
      introduction, 133-34
Introduction of a speech, 108,
    111-23
  analogy, 113-14
  anecdote, 115-16
  children's story or rhyme, 119-20
  gimmick, 122
  humor, 113
  hypothetical story, 117-18
  news story, 116-17
  object, 114-15
  provocative question, 112
  quotation, 120-21
  reference to a movie,
      television program, or
      play, 118-19

startling statement, 111-12
theme approach, 122-23
Isaacson, Max D., 16

J

Jacob, 9, 85
Jessel, George, 54
Jesus, 1-13, 57, 64, 65, 85-87,
    94, 110, 112, 115, 120-21,
    151, 158, 160, 218
Johnson, Lady Bird, 19
Johnson, Lyndon B., 211
Jones, Jenkin Lloyd, 135
Joseph, 93

K

Kennedy, John F., 15, 21, 66, 197
King, Jr., Martin Luther, 15, 57
Kiveloff, Dr. Boino, 22

L

Language, differences in oral
    and written, 55-56
Language, inclusive, 64-65
    Jesus' use of, 2-3
Larson, Muriel, 66
Lectern, 19, 24, 32, 35, 91, 95,
    131, 154
Length of speech, 129
Light openers for speeches, 208
Lincoln, Abraham, 56, 105, 129
Livner, Sandy, 54
Logophobia, 15

M

MacLachlan, James, 48
Magnet boards, 99-100
Mary, 3, 93

Master of ceremonies, 74, 137-40
Mathews, Alice, 64-65
Maxwell, Elsa, 79
McDowell, Josh, 78
Mechanics of speaking, 41-57, 133
Meeting Evaluation Form, 182
Meetings, 144, 177-188
    acoustics, 177
    arrangements, 177-78
    brainstorming, 182-84
    Checklist for Planning
        Meetings, 180
    conducting effectively, 179, 181
    guaranteed snafus, 187
    lighting, 177
    seating, 178-79
    types of participants, 184-87
Memorized speech, 175-76
Microphone, 32, 47, 62, 100-01,
    153, 191
Mikva, Abner J., 57
Miller, Calvin, 160
Mispronounced words, 51-52
Monotone, 21, 45
Monroe, Alan H., 78
Moody, Dwight L., 66
Mordecai, 154-56
Moses, 21, 85
Muir, Ken, 200

N

Nasality, 45
    exercises for, 45
National Speakers Association,
    The, 207
News conference, 162-63, 192-193
News interview, 193-202
    don'ts, 199-201
News media, 192-93

Nixon-Kennedy debate, 36
Notes, using, 32, 35, 37, 83, 90,
    94, 130-32

O

Object lesson, 10
Oral vs. written language, 55-
    56
Orben, Bob, 80
Overhead projectors, 91-92

P

Padding speech, 53-55
Paderewski, 25
Participation, audience, 61, 74-77
Pause, benefits, 48, 53-55
Persistence, 25
Persuasive speech, 143-45
Pitch, 42-46, 49
    effect of nervousness on,
        44, 49
    exercises, 44
    locating, 45
Posture, 27, 30-32
    seated, 31
    standing, 30-32
    unconscious habits, 32
    walking, 31-32
    with lectern, 32
    with microphone, 32
Preparing to speak, 129-35
    memorizing, 130-31
    using notes, 130-32
Presenting yourself as a
    speaker, 27-39
    appearance, 28-30
    eye contact, 35-37
    facial expressions, 37-39
    gestures, 32-35
    posture, 30-31

stage presence, 31-32
Projection, improving, 52
"Public Speaking and Other
    Coronary Threats", 16
Publications of help, 205-06
Pulpit presentation, 158-60

Q

Questions, 56, 68, 72, 75, 76, 81-
    84, 106, 108, 146, 112, 153,
    182, 187, 191, 194-95, 198
Question-and-answer session, 69,
    77, 81-84, 145-46, 148, 214
Questions of Jesus, 6-7, 112, 221

R

Range, vocal, 44, 45-46, 50, 204-05
Rate of delivery, *see Delivery rate*
Rehearsing, 132-33
    videotaping yourself, 133
Relaxation exercises, 22-23
Repetitive word or phrase, 54
Research speech, 146-48
Rhythm, 56-57, 109
Roast, 172-73
    example, 173-75
Rodman, Frances, 53
Roosevelt, Eleanor, 21
Rozakis, Laurie, 63, 111

S

Sarnoff, Dorothy, 53
Script, 37, 130, 154, 176
Scripture, Jesus' use of, 3-4
Scripture reading, 18, 120, 125,
    156-57, 159, 217-20
Seating arrangements, 61, 178, 188
Seating for banquet, 138

Shakespeare, William, 16, 33-34, 53, 121
Shaw, George Bernard, 25
Shocking statement, 10, 111, 219
  attention getter, 111
  in Scripture, 219
  Jesus' use of, 10
Silence, 48, 53-55, 171, 195, 200, 219
  benefits, 54
Simplicity, 28, 30, 105-06, 190
Skinner, Otis, 17
Slide projector, 94-95
Socrates, 11, 213
Speaking Engagement Information Form, 210
Speaking, mechanics of, 25, 42-57
Speech construction, 105-27
  body, 108-109, 124-25
  conclusion, 108, 125
  introduction, 108, 111
    analogy, 113
    anecdote, 115
    children's story or rhyme, 119
    gimmick, 122
    humor, 113,
    hypothetical story, 117
    make it personal, 119
    news story, 116
    object, 114
    provocative question, 112
    quote, 120
    reference to a movie, television program, or play, 118
    startling statement, 111

theme approach, 122
length, 62-63, 129-30
objective, 107
parts, 108
statement of purpose, 108, 123-24
statistics, 82, 125-26, 131, 147-48
supporting evidence, 125, 190
title, 108-10
transitions, 125, 150
using personal examples, 126
writing, 105-26
Speech of Introduction Outline Form, 142
Speech material files, 207
Speech Organization Form, 127
Speeches, types, 138-76
  commencement, 167
    example, 167-71
  dedication and commemoration, 163-64
    example, dedication, 165-67
  devotional, 156
    example, 157-58
  dramatic presentation, 153-54
    example, 154-56
  entertaining, 148-51
  impromptu, 160-62
  informative, 145-46
  introduction, 140-41
  memorized, 175-76
  persuasive, 143-45
  pulpit presentation, 158
  research, 146-48
  roast, 172-73
    example, 173-75
  storytelling, 151-53
  tribute or award, 171

example, 171-72
welcome or greeting, 162
example, 162-63
Stage fright, 15-26, 49, 79
bodily reactions, 17-18
ways to overcome, 18-23
Stage presence, 30-31
Statistics, 82, 117, 125-26, 127,
147-48, 190
Storytelling, 151-53

T

Tape recorder, 42-43, 51, 55, 94,
203-205
Taping yourself, 42-43
Television, 189-202
appearing on, 189-91
cautions, 191-92
during the production, 190-91
how to prepare, 190
what to wear, 189
Television as audiovisual aid, 97-98
Television, impact of, 27, 87, 112
Templeton, Charles, 84
Thielen, Martin, 113
Toastmasters International, 204,
206-207
Tribute speech, 171
example, 171-72
Trueblood, Elton, 12
Twain, Mark, 62, 162-63
Types of speeches, *see Speeches,
types*

V

Videotaping yourself, 133
Videocybernetics, 15
Visual aids, *see Audiovisual aids*
Vocal energy, 43

Vocal exercises, 44-45
Vocal level, 44, 46-47
microphone, 47
projecting, 43, 46, 62, 100
Vocal pitch, *see Pitch*
Vocal range, *see Range, vocal*
Voice, 42-50, 53-54, 94

W

Welcome speech, 162-163
examples, 64-65
White, E. B., 78
Wilcox, Roger P., 78
Wilde, Oscar, 79
Writing the speech, 105-27
Written vs. oral language, 55-56

Z

Zacchaeus, 3
Zechariah, 3
Zuck, Roy B., 8

Forms

Audience Analysis Form 70

Audiovisual Checklist 103

Checklist for Planning Meetings 180

Checklist for the Master of Ceremonies 139

Meeting Evaluation Form 182

Speaking Engagement Information Form 210

Speech of Introduction Outline Form 142

Speech Organization Form 127